Social Structure

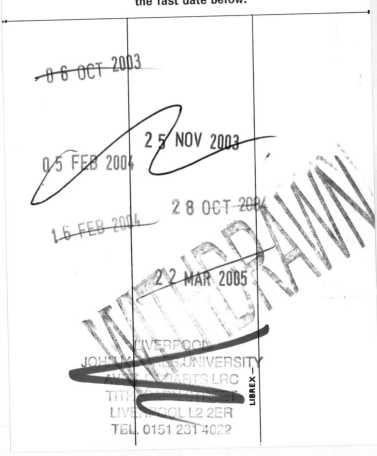

Current Titles

Concepts in the Social Sciences

Social Structure

José López and John Scott

Open University Press
Buckingham · Philadelphia

Open University Press
Celtic Court
22 Ballmoor
Buckingham
MK18 1XW

email: enquiries@openup.co.uk
world wide web: www.openup.co.uk

and

325 Chestnut Street
Philadelphia, PA 19106, USA

First Published 2000

A catalogue record of this book is available from the British Library

ISBN 0 335 20495 3 (pb)   0 335 20496 1 (hb)

Library of Congress Cataloging-in-Publication Data
López, José, 1966–
    Social structure / José López and John Scott.
        p.   cm. — (Concepts in the social sciences)
    Includes bibliographical references and index.
    ISBN 0-335-20495-3 (pb) — ISBN 0-335-20496-1 (hb)
    1. Social structure.   2. Social institutions.   3.   Sociology.
    I. Scott, John, 1949–   II. Title.   III. Series.

HM706.L67   2000
306—dc21   00-035624

Typeset by Type Study, Scarborough
Printed in Great Britain by St Edmundsbury Press, Bury St Edmunds

Contents

What is Social Structure?

'Social structure' has always been one of the central concepts in sociological theory and analysis. Indeed, it has now become some-thing of a commonplace to see the major disputes of contemporary sociology as organized around the dualism of 'structure' and 'action'. While there have been many discussions of the nature and meaning of social action, there have been very few definitional works on social structure. Indeed, social structure is usually treated as a taken-for-granted concept that is not in need of any explicit definition or discussion. Actual uses of the concept, however, are strikingly nebulous and diverse. As a result, there is little consensus over what the word means, and it is all too easy for sociologists to be talking at cross purposes because they rely on different, and generally implicit, conceptions of social structure.

This peculiar situation – that one of the discipline's central con-cepts is so misunderstood – is clear from the definitions of social structure that are given in the leading dictionaries of sociology. One of the most important of these defines social structure as 'A term loosely applied to any recurring pattern of social behaviour; or, more specifically, to the ordered interrelationships between the different elements of a social system or society' (Concise Oxford Dictionary of Sociology 1994: 517). Having given this very general characterization, the dictionary disarmingly adds, 'However, there is no generally agreed meaning, and attempts at providing succinct definitions have proved singularly unsuccessful.' In a strikingly similar way, another dictionary holds that social structure is 'Any relatively enduring pattern or interrelationship of social elements ... The more or less enduring patterns of social arrangements within a particular society' (Collins' Dictionary of Sociology 1991:

597). This dictionary entry, too, goes on to say that 'No single concept of social structure exists in sociology, despite its widespread usage.'

These dictionary definitions have undoubtedly highlighted the central idea behind the use of the word 'structure': it is a pattern or arrangement of elements. They further show that a specifically *social* structure is a pattern or arrangement of the elements of a society. But this does not get us very far, as it tells us neither what the elements are, nor how the patterns are sustained. What does it mean to talk about a 'pattern' of social behaviour, and exactly where do we find the pattern as opposed to the behaviour itself?

Our aim in this book is to draw out the concepts of social structure that have actually been employed in sociological discussions. We want to make both clear and explicit a concept that has come to be not only vague and implicit, but also highly contested. We think that this task can be facilitated by drawing on the analysis or 'history of concepts' developed by Bachelard (1937), Canguilhem (1968, 1977) and Foucault (1971). Although these authors engaged in different substantive areas (Bachelard in physics and mathematics, Canguilhem in the life sciences and Foucault in the human sciences), and developed distinctive methodologies, they nonetheless shared some core assumptions concerning the analysis of scientific concepts.

In the first place, the meaning of a concept cannot be determined with reference to everyday language; its meaning has to be understood in the context of the conceptual or discursive networks in which it is embedded and used. Consequently, we will not simply pick on each and every use of the *term* 'social structure'. The term has sometimes, for example, been used to refer to statistical patterns and distributions such as those reported in demographic and economic investigations (Marsh 1961). This use, however, trades on the scientific value of the idea of 'structure' without developing any conceptual understanding of it. In contrast, we seek to explore the various conceptual frameworks within which ideas of social structure have been formulated, showing how the assumptions made in these frameworks have shaped the ways in which social structure is understood.

Second, a concept is not a theory. A concept in itself is not an explanation. Instead, a good concept demarcates a phenomenon of interest so that theoretical explanatory strategies can be developed. Thus although concepts are integrated in theories, their meanings

cannot be merely derived from knowledge of, or the logical architecture of, a theory. In fact, it is possible to have a number of com-
peting theories using the same concept (Gutting 1989: 34), as it is
also possible to have concepts that are not properly integrated with
other concepts in a theory. Thus concepts have a relative autonomy
from the logical structure of the theories in which they are embedded. We believe that the analytical importance of this is that a
history of a concept, as well as its associated meanings, need not be
understood merely in terms of a history of theoretical traditions –
though, as we will show, they often do cluster around them.

As we see it, 'social structure' and its associated terms have most
typically been used as ways of describing the *organization* of social
life, just as structural thinking in other disciplines has been moti-
vated by attempts to theorize the specific forms of organization that
define their subject matters. Thus, there can be structural analyses
of physical phenomena, chemical phenomena, mental phenomena,
and, of course, social phenomena. Our focus is on concepts of social
structure, and we seek to elucidate the various concepts that have
been employed – in whatever terminology – to grasp the structural
aspects of social life. If 'structure' is to be understood, for the
moment, to mean pattern or arrangement – as opposed to that
which is 'random' or 'chaotic' – then our aim is to see in exactly
what ways the pattern or arrangement of social life has been understood.

We will show that the history of sociology shows the long-term
coexistence of two different conceptions of social structure. On the
one hand, there is that which we identify as the idea of *institutional
structure*. Here, social structure is seen as comprising those cultural
or normative patterns that define the expectations that agents hold
about each other's behaviour and that organize their enduring
relations with each other. On the other hand, there is the idea of
what we call *relational structure*. Here, social structure is seen as
comprising the social relations themselves, understood as patterns
of causal interconnection and interdependence among agents and
their actions, as well as the positions that they occupy.

Debates in theoretical and empirical sociology have, in large part,
been shaped by the rivalry between advocates of these two different concepts of social structure. Advocates of institutional structure
and of relational structure have sometimes seen their preferred idea
as being the *only* valid concept of social structure to employ. More
typically, however, there has been simply a difference of emphasis.

Those who have emphasized institutional structure have tended to see relational structure as being of secondary and, perhaps, derivative importance, while those who have emphasized relational structure have seen institutional structure as the secondary factor.

We do not think it is useful or sensible to propound either of these claims at such a general level. As we highlighted above, concepts are not rigorously defined by theoretical strategies. In fact the meaning of a concept is never entirely closed, as post-structuralists have rightly argued.[1] As a result, in trying to uncover the meaning of the concept of social structure, we will show that the concept has more depth and that its meanings are more diverse than is often revealed in discussions of it. The concept of social structure points to a complex articulation of the institutional and relational elements of social life. The relative importance of the two aspects of social structure is something that will vary from one situation to another and about which it is impossible to generalize. What is quite clearly implied by this view, however, is the belief that analyses of institutional structure and relational structure offer *complementary*, not alternative, frameworks of sociological analysis. Sociology will prosper only if it recognizes this.

Recently, however, new understandings of social structure have come to challenge these established views. Inspired by developments in theoretical linguistics, anthropology and, more recently, evolutionary psychology, a new conceptual framework has made itself felt in sociological debates. Those working within this intellectual context have argued that social structure must be seen as analogous to the grammatical structures of speech and texts. According to this point of view, patterns of institutions and relations result from the actions of individuals who are endowed with the capacities or competencies that enable them to produce them by acting in organized ways. These capacities are behavioural dispositions, and so social structure has to be seen as an *embodied structure*. Embodied structures are found in the habits and skills that are inscribed in human bodies and minds and that allow them to produce, reproduce, and transform institutional structures and relational structures.

Proponents of the idea of embodied structure have tended to see it as being the most fundamental aspect of social structure. Indeed, many have denied that there is any other kind of social structure at all. For those who work within post-structuralism and post-modernism, for example, grand narratives of social structure – along with those other grand narratives of society and social system – must be abandoned (Lemert 1998). They hold that there is no whole or totality separate from the *structuring* activities and practices that are engaged in by individual actors.

Our view is, again, that this is too extreme. Institutional structures and relational structures do depend, as we will show, on embodied structures, but this does not make them any the less real. Social structure, in our view, is a concept that points to three interdependent aspects of the organization of social life: the institutional, the relational, and the embodied. The power of sociological analysis lies in the recognition of this. Those approaches that have emphasized one aspect to the exclusion of all others tend to lose their intellectual power and vitality. The complementarity of the three aspects of social structure, and the need to work with them all, must be kept firmly at the centre of sociological attention.

This view should not be taken as implying any priority for 'structure' over 'action'. The supposed incompatibility of these two ideas is overstated, and the suggestion that sociological researchers must choose between them is misguided. Social structures, as we will show, depend on the existence of human beings that act and exercise agency. However, they cannot be reduced to these actions, and so they cannot be eliminated from sociological analysis. At the same time, of course, actions are always and necessarily structured by the social contexts in which they occur. There can be no action without structure (Archer 1995).

The duality of action and structure in sociological debate is, at most, a reflection of an intellectual division of labour, a methodological 'bracketing' of one set of concerns in order to concentrate on another. In this book, we bracket off questions of action and agency in order to concentrate on those of social structure. But this must be recognized for the methodological convenience that it is. No ultimate priority of structure over action is implied.

We have organized our discussion of social structure around the three aspects that we have identified. Chapter 3 looks at institutional structure, Chapter 4 at relational structure, and Chapter 6 at embodied structure. In Chapter 5 we examine those views of social structure that have been concerned with attempting to represent its ontological depth or levels of social complexity. These views are clustered around three conceptual frameworks: base/superstructure, system/subsystem and social fields. We will show that an understanding of the possibilities contained in this facet of social structure is another crucial element in the development of concepts that are capable of capturing the complex organization that constitutes social life.

In Chapter 2 we trace the emergence and establishment of structural thinking in a range of scientific disciplines, tracing the sequences of uses through which the meaning of 'structure' was gradually refined and then applied within the emerging discipline of sociology in the nineteenth century. We look, in particular, at the ways in which these ideas were explored in the works of Spencer and Durkheim, whose discussions of social structure set the scene for all that followed.

A developmental approach informs our discussions in each of the other chapters, though we have deliberately avoided presenting the work of the writers that we discuss as a sequence of schools of thought. We attempt to present a history of the concept of structure, which is not the same as a history of social thought. We also do not provide a sociology of sociology, in which modes of thought are constantly related to the social and historical contexts that give birth to them. In sum, we do not try to relate concepts of social structure exclusively to particular traditions of social thought, to the works of particular geniuses, or to particular historical periods. We aim to show how the concepts have arisen in diverse schools and in the works of a wide range of authors. On the other hand, we do not want to imply that the emergence and development of sociological ideas can be seen simply as the cumulative outcome of a subjectless process. Both the history of social thought and the sociology of sociology are important approaches to knowledge, but our aim in this book is different. It is a contribution to debates over social structure that derives much support from these concerns, but which, ultimately, aims to present intellectually coherent accounts of the various concepts of social structure and to demonstrate their contemporary relevance to the sociological debates of today.

2

Conceptualizing Social Structure

We have argued that debates over the concept of social structure can be more fruitfully pursued by making explicit the conceptual networks from which the different uses of the concept obtain their meaning. In doing so, however, it is important to realize that the concept of 'structure' had its own history before it was used to conceptualize social organization. Having reviewed this history, we will go on to show how these networks of concepts were used by nineteenth-century writers to gradually build a picture of what they variously called the 'social organism' or the 'social mind'. We will look, in particular, at the works of the two leading writers to present systematic accounts of social structure: Herbert Spencer and Emile Durkheim. This will not only clarify their use of the concept of social structure or organization. It will also show how the conceptual networks from which they drew their concepts allowed them to make important theoretical innovations while at the same time constraining what they could say.

'Structure' before 'social structure'

The English word 'structure' derives from the Latin word *struere*, to build. The – *ure* ending is used in English to form nouns that denote an action or a process, or that refer to the result or outcome of a process. Hence, 'structure' can mean 'building' in both of its principal senses. It can mean the act of building something, and it can mean the end product of a building process. Its core meaning, therefore, is related to that of other words such as 'constructing' and 'forming'. The word was widely used in this sense in the fifteenth century to refer to an actual physical building or edifice (such as a house or a cathedral) and also to the principles behind its construction. This latter usage pointed to the balance of forces that gave the building its particular shape or form. The term 'structure', therefore, specifically implied the inner arrangement, composition or organization of the constituent elements of a building. A structure was a building or edifice that owed its distinctive characteristics to the fact that its parts were organized in some specific way.

'Structure' retained this range of meaning through much of the seventeenth and eighteenth centuries, its main usage being in practical architecture and the science of geometry that explored the abstract mathematical properties of different kinds of structure. The massive growth of the physical sciences, however, involved an extension of the concept into new scientific areas. Hooke, for example, looked at the forces of tension and compression that result from the changes in shape that a structure undergoes when subjected to a load. He distinguished 'elastic' structures, that recover their shape when a load is removed, from 'plastic' structures that do not. In the nineteenth century, Cauchy made the first significant advance on Hooke's work when he introduced the concepts of 'stress' and 'strain' to investigate the elasticity and plasticity of structures. These novel ideas were responsible for the massive strides that were made in engineering during the nineteenth and twentieth centuries, as the mechanics of tension structures and compression structures were applied to the construction of such things as bridges, ships, aircraft, and 'skyscraper' blocks.

The extension of structural ideas from architecture to engineering encouraged their use in other scientific disciplines. During the nineteenth century, the word 'structure' came to be used in biology to refer to a combination of connected and interdependent parts that make up an organism. The wing of a bird and the leg of a mammal, for example, were seen as particular, specialized structures. Whole organized bodies – organisms – were seen as complex organized combinations of organs and other elements, and they could themselves be seen as biological structures.

At around this same time, 'structure' was also beginning to be used in geology to describe the patterns of rock formation that make up the earth's crust and surface layers, and in chemistry to describe the arrangement of atoms into molecules. The word 'structure', then, was coming to be seen as a technical, scientific term that could be used in a whole variety of fields to describe the arrangement of the parts of any complex, organized whole into a specific pattern or form.

Much of this structural thought, however, was purely static, treating structures as timeless Platonic forms. There was little idea of the development or transformation of structures. This was true even in biology. Richard Owen was, by the 1840s, the leading exponent of the idea that different forms of life could be grouped according to similarities in their anatomy and physiology and that the various groups could each be related to one of a small number of archetypal structures. The members of each group could, furthermore, be arranged in a sequence from lower to higher levels of organization relative to their archetype. What he and those influenced by him would not accept was the idea that these were sequences of evolution in which one structure could develop or transform itself into another. If cathedrals did not transform themselves into bridges, why should it be believed that one species could evolve into another?

Darwin, of course, was to supply precisely the reason why this should be believed, firmly linking the idea of structure to that of development. Support for developmental ideas had been growing in geology and biology through the nineteenth century, from Lamarck through Lyell to Spencer, but no one had yet provided a clear picture of the mechanism that could make the transmutation of structure possible. Although Darwin felt that he had discovered a solution to this problem by the 1830s, he kept this knowledge secret until he felt that it could be published without being rejected out of hand by the religious orthodoxy. Publication of *The Origin of Species* in 1859 finally showed that structural development was possible not only within the lifetime of a particular individual, but also across sequences of species. Structural analysis could, then, be dynamic as well as static (Thompson 1917).

It was in this conceptual and theoretical context that the pioneer sociologists began to grapple with the idea of *social* structure. The notion that societies could be regarded as organized wholes can, of course, be traced back at least as far as Plato and Aristotle, but it was not until the rapid development of the natural sciences in the seventeenth and eighteenth centuries that this became a common way of approaching the social world. The physical, chemical and biological sciences were seen as having made great strides by focusing on their characteristic subject matters and adopting a structural approach to their study. Many began to feel that a science of society could be achieved through the same means. Comte, for example, saw each of these sciences as showing a progressively higher level of organization in its subject matter. There was a hierarchy of sciences, with sociology being the last to develop because of the particularly complex nature of the organization of its subject matter.

Early sociology borrowed many ideas from the more advanced natural sciences, and these sciences, in turn, not infrequently borrowed them back. Thus, Condorcet sought to explore the mathematical aspects of social structure, while Claude Bernard, and others, explored physiology on the analogy of 'society'. These shared ideas were not necessarily seen as 'borrowing' or 'imitating' at all, as structural ideas of organization and complexity had come to be seen as common features of the scientific worldview, in both the natural and the social sciences (Vergata 1994).

The attempt to theorize a distinctively *social* form of organization through the concept of social structure threw up a problem that has remained a contentious point of debate in the human sciences until the present. This is the question of whether a social structure has an existence independent of the individual human beings that are its ultimate elements. This arose because social and mental structures seemed to have a slightly different character from those of architecture, physics and biology. In all the areas in which the word 'structure' had been used until the middle of the nineteenth century, structures were either visible or, in principle, observable. They could actually be seen, with or without the aid of instruments of observation. This was not the case in the newly expanding sciences of psychology and sociology: neither mental processes nor social institutions were observable independently of the individuals who held them or produced them. Spencer, for example, held that structures of interdependence in social life, no matter how real, were not material entities and so could not be directly observed. They could be studied only through inference and through the observation of their consequences.

The non-observability of social structures meant that, initially, sociologists were very vague about precisely *what* social structure was thought to be. It seemed possible to talk about social structure as the arrangement or pattern among the parts of a society, without specifying what these parts were (other than individual human beings) and how the patterns were formed. Attempts to conceptualize social structure drew on two metaphors in an effort to grasp this complexity. On the one hand, a social structure was seen as akin to a biological organism and as forming a social body or *social organism*. On the other hand, it was seen as akin to a personality or soul and as forming a *social mind*. For those who preferred to talk of the social organism, it was natural to focus on the material interdependence, division of labour and exchange among individuals and the ways in which the 'anatomy' of social life could be explored. Those who used the metaphor of the social mind, on the other hand, focused on the communication of ideas among individuals and the ways in which the 'spirit' of a society shaped its constituent members.

The most influential of those who talked of the social organism was Schäffle, whose *Structure and Life of Social Bodies* (1875–80) saw social systems as organized around differentiated functional structures that operated in analogous ways to the brain, the heart, and the stomach in living organisms. The central organ in any social organism, he held, is the system of national economy, the economic system. This is a 'social process of digestion', a 'digestive apparatus' that produces means of subsistence and excretes material waste.

The idea of the social mind, on the other hand, was forwarded most systematically by Hegel. Mind, or spirit, he held, was the element of 'ideality' that distinguished the human from the merely external world of nature or matter, and Hegel distinguished the 'subjective mind' studied by psychology from the 'objective mind' studied by the socio-historical sciences of ethics and law. Norms, rules and customs are the elements of this objective mind and are expressed in the institutions of family, civil society, and state. The state itself he saw as 'an organized whole' that operates as 'a living mind' (Hegel 1807: 265).

These were the conceptual and theoretical networks that constrained and made possible Spencer and Durkheim's explicit and systematic formulations of structural ideas in sociology. Notwithstanding the many inadequacies of their formulations, they articulated a basic view of social structure that remains with us today.

Spencer and the social organism

Though he was not in any direct sense a follower of Comte, it was Herbert Spencer who first set out an explicit discussion of social structure along Comtean lines. It was his delineation of the sphere of the social that proved highly influential among those who were to establish the foundations of classical sociology. While continuing to base his arguments on the Hobbesian image of the individual that he shared with Mill and the classical political economists, Spencer also set out a model of the 'social organism'. This he understood as resulting from the rational, calculative interactions of individuals, but as having definite properties and characteristics of its own.

The social organism and the biological organism have, according to Spencer, many common characteristics. In particular, they both have a permanency in the arrangement of their parts: they show a constancy or fixity of *structure*. Both social structures and biological structures, furthermore, are to be seen as the outcome of processes of growth or development (Spencer 1876: 436). In the case of the social organism, structural development results from the interplay of the actions of the constituent individuals. This is not to say, of course, that it has to be seen as a conscious and deliberate creation of these individuals. Spencer shared with Adam Smith and the other writers of the Scottish Enlightenment the view that social conditions had to be understood as the unintended and unplanned outcome of individual actions.

It is the fact that the elements of a social organism are sentient individuals that gives it the characteristics that distinguish it from any biological organism. While the cells from which biological organisms are built are physically connected to each other, 'the men who make up a society, are physically separate and even scattered' (Spencer 1864: 394). Direct physical connection is rare in social life. Only in relations of sex and violence is there any direct flow of energy or vital fluids or any direct physical influence among individuals. Human individuals are, rather, connected through language – and even sex and violence must be seen as linguistically organized behaviours. It is the linguistic communication of signs from one person to another that allows them to transfer emotion and information. In living bodies, impulses are conveyed from unit to unit by 'molecular waves'. In societies, causal influence occurs through 'the signs of feelings and thoughts, conveyed from person to person' (Spencer 1876: 448). Language, Spencer argued, is the 'inter-nuncial', or message carrying, channel of the social organism. It is a container and conveyor of information and emotion, and it is what makes social structure possible. It is this recognition that helped Spencer's concept of the social organism to incorporate many of those features that others saw in the social mind. The social organism has to be seen as a mental phenomenon as much as a material one.

How, then, did Spencer see social structures? He said first of all that they are not to be seen as material entities. A social organism does not form a 'continuous mass' in any material sense. He also held that 'societies have no specific external forms', no skeletons, shells, or fleshy substances of their own. They are discontinuous, discrete, and dispersed, manifest only in myriad individuals and the material objects that they use in their actions. For this reason, social structures are not directly visible or available for direct inspection in the same way as a physically existent biological organism (Spencer 1873: 73).

It was in Chapter 4 of his *Principles of Sociology* that Spencer gave his most extended discussion of social structure. While whole societies are to be considered as complex social structures, he gave particular attention to the internal organization of societies into more specialized social structures. Such social structures, he argued, are sub-aggregates of individuals within a social organism. They are 'clustered citizens' (Spencer 1876: 466) that differ in some socially significant way from the other members of their society. These social structures are analogous to the organs of a living body in so far as they tend to be more or less specialized in particular tasks or activities. These tasks are the 'functions' that they undertake. A whole society, then, is a set of connected structures, a 'system of organs'.

Spencer went on to describe the various social structures that he thought were the elements of whole societies. These he termed the sustaining, distributing, and regulating structures of the social organism. However, he said nothing more about the defining characteristics of social structures as general phenomena in social life. His analysis of linguistically mediated communication as the means through which social structures are produced was suggestive, but undeveloped. His ideas had to be thoroughly reworked before they could yield a viable account of social structure. This reworking was undertaken by Durkheim.

Durkheim: relationships and representations

Durkheim used the word 'social structure' relatively rarely in his work. When he did so, it was to refer to the overall pattern of social life in societies studied as wholes. He saw tribal and modern societies, for example, as distinct social types or 'social species', characterized, respectively, by 'mechanical solidarity' and 'organic solidarity' (Durkheim 1893). In describing these various forms of social structure, however, Durkheim gave little detail about their precise constitution. In his exploration of the general character of what he called 'social facts', however, he defined 'collective relationships' and 'collective representations' as the elements from which social structures are built. Together with the 'morphological' features of social life in which they are grounded, he argued, these are the 'social facts' with which sociologists must be concerned.[1]

Social facts, Durkheim held, are those ways of acting, thinking, and feeling that are general throughout a particular society and that are able to exercise an 'external constraint' over its members (Durkheim 1895). Individuals are born into a world of social facts that pre-exist them and that, in many cases, will persist for long after they have died. A pattern of kinship relations (mother, father, son, daughter, etc.), the grammar and vocabulary of a language, a system of money and prices, and a network of roads and railways all have these characteristics. They are general, external and enduring. External social facts constrain individuals in many different ways. They may limit their abilities to act in certain ways, open up new opportunities, or evoke a sense of obligation and commitment among those who have been fully socialized into the ways of their society. A language, for example, limits and channels the ways in which people can speak, while a network of roads limits and channels the ways in which they move about in their cars. Similarly, moral commitments to kinship roles create a sense of obligation that predisposes people to care for family members, while trust in a monetary system obliges them to accept pieces of metal and paper in exchange for goods and services.

Durkheim began his analysis of social facts with an exploration of what he called the 'morphological facts' in which they are visible. Morphological facts result from 'the mass of individuals who constitute society, the manner in which they have settled upon the earth, the nature and configuration of those things of all kinds which affect collective relationships' (Durkheim 1895: 57). Morphological facts include the size and density of a population in its territory; its distribution across urban and rural areas; forms of building and architecture; patterns of transport, boundaries, and frontiers; the distribution of natural resources; and the technologies that are produced by using those resources. These facts are all to be considered as aspects of the material ecology and natural environment within which individuals find themselves and that they transform through their social activities. Morphological facts are the specialized concern of geography and demography, which Durkheim saw, in this respect, as disciplines ancillary to sociology.

Morphological facts do not themselves constitute social structures, Durkheim argued. They are, rather, a 'substructure', a foundation upon which the social structure proper is built. They are, however, the only external and tangible forms in which other social facts appear and have their effects. As Spencer recognized, the social bond that connects individuals is not a material bond, though it can be inferred only indirectly from its external, material forms. From this delineation of social morphology, Durkheim went on to discuss the characteristics of social structure proper.

'Collective relationships' – social relations – constitute the first aspect of social structure that he identified. They depend upon particular morphological conditions, and they may be visible through them, but they remain separate and quite distinct from them. They are what Durkheim termed the 'internal social milieu' of a society, as opposed to its external, morphological milieu, and define forms of attachment among individuals. Kinship relations, for example, depend upon the existence of physical individuals with particular reproductive capacities and patterns of ageing, and they are made visible or more tangible in a distribution of housing types and households, and in the concentration and dispersal of a population. Nevertheless, the kinship relations themselves are irreducible to these demographic conditions and they must be studied directly and independently by sociologists.

Social relations cluster into distinct patterns, and these can be considered as the 'parts' of a society. Such structural parts as the systems of morality, economy, kinship and the state were, for Durkheim as for Spencer, analogous to the organs of the body. They are differentiated and specialized sets of social relations that have a particular 'function' within the whole society, just as differentiated physiological organs have their particular functions within the body. Societies, then, are social bodies with an 'anatomy' of social relations and a 'physiology' of functional connections.

'Collective representations' constitute a second aspect of social structure. Collective representations are mental phenomena, and Durkheim held that all mental phenomena, to the extent that they are not the direct and unique products of individual biology, are to be seen as social facts.[2] They are the beliefs, ideas, values, symbols, and expectations that exist only in the minds of individuals, but that can be communicated from one individual to another and that regulate their behaviour. It is through this process of communication that representations come to be shared and, therefore, to be held more or less generally throughout a society. The 'social consciousness', then, is the total stock of collective representations that is created through the processes of socialization and imitation that make up the larger process of social communication.

Like collective relationships, collective representations can become visible or tangible in some external, material form. Ideas can be written down or published in letters, books, and newspapers; laws can be printed in official documents; and musical ideas can be recorded on to tapes and disks. These documentary embodiments of the collective representations, however, are not to be confused with the representations themselves. They are merely material indicators of the collective representations. It is only when a written idea is read, and enters the minds of the readers, that it has the power to constrain their actions, thoughts, and feelings by providing them with a mental pattern or a sense of obligation. Collective representations, therefore, are distinct and separate from their material expressions. They form an autonomous sphere of mental objects. If collective relationships can be said to form a social body, collective representations can be said to form a social mind or mentality. At its strongest, Durkheim saw this as forming a 'collective conscience', a core of representations that are 'common to the average members' of a society (Durkheim 1893: 38–9, 64). Durkheim sometimes suggested that collective representations form a completely separate level, a superstructure that arises above the structure of social relations.

The social structure of a society, then, consists of the particular complex of collective relationships and collective representations, forms of attachment and regulation, that give the society its specific characteristics. For example, a simple and undifferentiated tribal society forms a structure of mechanical solidarity in so far as there is a high level of consensus, and the collective conscience, as a result, exercises a strong compelling power over the actions, thoughts, and feelings of its members. The individual is completely absorbed or engulfed by the social mind. Each member is similar to all the others – they have no individual identity – and their social

relations can be completely governed by their shared representations. In these circumstances, social action is characterized by
conformity, altruism, and fatalism.

In modern societies, on the other hand, individuals are far more
differentiated from one another. Each follows a specialized pattern
of activity. The collective conscience is less relevant in relation to
these specialized activities and shrinks to a relatively small core.
There is much greater diversity in the collective representations
that make up the current social stock of ideas, and there is, in consequence, a much greater scope for individual choice of action.
Each person draws on collective representations that are shared
with those performing the same task, but that are not shared with
all other members of their society. Social action, in these circumstances, is characterized by a high level of institutionalized individualism. Social life can no longer be regulated by a monolithic
collective conscience, and more specifically relational mechanisms
are required. In such a situation, Durkheim argued, individuals are
integrated through bonds of organic solidarity, in which it is the
interdependence of each upon all others that ties them together. In
these circumstances, there is the ever-present danger that this
normal individualism will degenerate into one of the 'pathological'
states of egoism and anomie, where individuality is unconstrained
and unregulated by collective relationships.

Durkheim's work has inspired, directly or indirectly, most of the
leading approaches to structural sociology. In the rest of this book,
we will first explore Durkheim's two aspects of social structure: collective relationships and collective representations. We will show,
however, that they have inspired quite different traditions of
thought, and only rarely have they been brought together in a single
theory. Relational ideas had their greatest impact through Radcliffe-Brown and the British social anthropologists, and through
ideas derived from Simmel and Tönnies. For these writers, sociological analysis was to be concerned with the networks of social
relations that tied people together into groups and larger social
systems. In the work of Parsons and the structural functionalists, on
the other hand, relational ideas were all but reduced to a residual
status. These writers focused on the structures of collective representations, which they termed social institutions. In a different
form, this orientation lay behind American cultural anthropology,
which combined it with a Hegelian awareness of the 'patterns of
culture' that define forms of social organization. The concern of

these writers was with the ways in which social relations are normatively patterned. Both *relational structure* and *institutional structure*, then, have their origins in the sociology of Durkheim, but they
have been developed largely independently of one another.

However, as we highlighted above, Durkheim understood social
structure proper as a complex articulation of both *institutional*
and *relational* structures. Consequently his influence can also be
detected in the predominantly French tradition (including Mauss,
Lévi-Strauss, Foucault, and Bourdieu) that has been concerned
with linking these two facets of social structure. This conceptual
and theoretical legacy is best exemplified in the work of Bourdieu
and Foucault. Finally, Durkheim's concern with morphological
facts, and the different modalities of the distribution of individuals
in social space, can also be detected in Foucault's conception of
social structure which links *embodied* structure to the organization
of the social body.

3
Institutional Structure

In Chapter 2, we showed that Durkheim's work combined two distinct concepts of social structure. These were the collective relationships that form relational structures and the collective representations that give rise to institutional structures. In this chapter we look at institutional structure, and we turn to relational structure in Chapter 4.

An appreciation of the importance of institutional structure can be found in many traditions of sociological analysis, but its clearest and most systematic expression was in the social thought of Talcott Parsons and other structural functionalist theorists. Their work on social structure, allied with the concept of 'function', produced an intellectual synthesis that, from the 1940s to the 1960s, formed the mainstream of sociological analysis. The core ideas on institutional structure that they set out, however, can be separated from the wider framework of 'functionalism', and they were widely accepted by sociologists who were otherwise very critical of structural functionalism.

Parsons constructed his institutionalist account of social structure in a series of essays written in the 1940s, and he also transmitted these ideas to others through his teaching at Harvard. From 1931 until his retirement, Parsons taught a course on comparative social institutions that latterly went under the title of 'Institutional Structure' (Parsons 1971a: 279). His leading students – Robert Merton, Bernard Barber, Kingsley Davis, and Marion Levy – diffused these ideas more widely as they pursued their careers in postwar sociology.

Parsons and his students have often been described as normative functionalists because they saw institutional structure as formed from shared 'norms'. These norms, in turn, were seen as based in a value consensus. It is undoubtedly true that they overemphasized normative and value consensus, and minimized the part that is played by conflict and contention over social values (Wrong 1961). This criticism does not, however, require an abandonment of the concept of institutional structure itself. So-called conflict theorists, for example, sought to detach the concept from the consensus assumption – and from its wider 'functionalist' framework – and to recognize the part played by power in sustaining norms and social institutions. Ralf Dahrendorf's (1957) analysis of social institutions, for example, owed as much to Weber and Marx as it did to Parsons and Durkheim. Robert Merton, Edward Shils, and Shmuel Eisenstadt ploughed increasingly independent furrows that owed a great deal to both normative functionalism and conflict theory, and they made a number of important contributions to the analysis of institutional structure. Thus it is possible to identify a set of conceptual networks and theoretical strategies through which Parsons, and his critics represented social organization in terms of institutional structure.

Theoretical challenges to structural functionalism broadened out during the 1960s and 1970s into increasingly vociferous rejections of the idea of social structure itself. For many sociologists, 'action' and/or 'practice' had to be placed at the centre of intellectual attention. We will look at the implications of this view in Chapter 6. For the present, however, it is necessary to point out the renewed attention that has been given to institutional structure since the 1980s. Recent work by 'neofunctionalists' such as Jefferey Alexander, Niklas Luhmann, and Richard Münch, supported by the later work of Neil Smelser, has restated the importance of attempts to theorize institutional structure. Similarly, the so-called new institutionalism that has taken root in economics, political science, and organizational studies has helped to renew a focus on institutional structure. The area of institutional structure has traditionally been concerned with examining institutions at the national, and sometimes subnational, level. However, recent scholarship has emphasized the importance of considering also the transnational dimension of institutional structure. Although these approaches have in some sense not formed part of mainstream sociology (cultural and post-colonial theorists, for example, have often positioned themselves in opposition to the so-called modernist sociology of Parsons), they nonetheless highlight the importance of thinking about and conceptualizing cultural patterns of behaviour. In this chapter, we draw on these theoretical approaches and their conceptual universes to argue that any structural account of societies must incorporate an understanding of the operation of institutional structures.

The cultural background

Social institutions have their basis in the culture that people share as members of a community or society. They are, at heart, cultural phenomena. The particular concept of culture adopted by Parsons and his school was developed in the early years of the twentieth century by Franz Boas and those who sought to establish models of 'culture and personality'. The key figures were Edward Sapir, Ruth Benedict (1934), Alfred Kroeber, and Ralph Linton (1945), as well as Boas himself. A related influence on this emerging idea was Malinowski's functionalist view of culture (Parsons 1957; Richards 1957). These writers shared a view of culture as a 'superorganic' phenomenon (Kroeber 1917), a symbolic realm that went beyond the merely organic.

Culture is what makes human beings distinctively human. It consists of the beliefs, ideas, sentiments, and symbols – in short, the collective representations – that people share. It is a patterned system of symbols that mediate and regulate communication (Parsons 1951: 327).[1] Culture includes the whole body of knowledge that people hold in common and the various ideas and values that provide them with general principles for action, rules of behaviour, and legitimating beliefs. It is transmitted from person to person through communication, and it is acquired by new members of society (infants and children) through socialization. Individual personalities are formed through the 'internalization' of cultural ideas, and this internalization ensures a degree of uniformity in the personality or 'character' of those who live in particular societies (Kroeber and Kluckhohn 1952).

It is within individual minds, then, that culture exists. The culture of a society is an abstraction that is identified by the sociologist or anthropologist from the contents of individual minds and the artefacts that people produce (Linton 1945: 28–9). In Kluckhohn's words, a culture is 'the network of abstracted patterns generalized by the anthropologist to represent the regularities distinctive of the group in question' (Kluckhohn 1954: 924). As such, it has no substantial existence outside individual minds and the mental processes that inform their actions. Nevertheless, culture is not a purely subjective reality. As collective representations, cultural entities also have an objective reality. This is not the reality of a social or group mind, but the reality of a system of shared values and ideas.[2] As Durkheim recognized, collective representations are regular, general, and enduring within a society and, therefore, can be studied *as if* they exist externally to individuals. Indeed, they can be seen as 'external' precisely because individuals themselves perceive them as objective and external facts.

Margaret Archer has recently cast this in more abstract terms: a cultural system is a 'corpus of existing intelligibilia', a collection of 'things capable of being grasped, deciphered, understood, or known' (Archer 1988: 104. See also Jarvie 1972). The relations among the elements that make up a culture are not relations of 'real interconnection', of causal or functional connection. The coherence of a culture is a matter of the 'internal relations between meaning components' (Habermas 1981b: 226). These internal relations are those of logic, rationality, and stylistic resemblance.[3] A particular scientific discipline, for example, comprises a network of concepts, propositions, models, and laws that stand in meaningful and often logical relations to one another. Similarly, a language is a system of sounds or graphic marks that is connected to a system of meanings through grammatical and semantic rules.[4]

Whether the coherence of a culture is understood in terms of logic, rules, rationality, or thematic and stylistic unity, the underlying idea is that there is a conceptual or meaningful 'pattern consistency' in cultural objects that is quite different from any subjective consistency that they may have in individual minds. The sociological task is to explore what Benedict has called the 'patterns of culture' (Benedict 1934. See also Parsons 1945a: 229, 1951: 15), and to show how these can become integrated with the interests and motives of individuals.

Social institutions are cultural phenomena, and this preamble on culture has been necessary to bring out the fact that the institutional patterns that comprise a social structure have the same virtual existence as all other cultural phenomena. To explore this further, we can now turn to the idea of the social institution itself.

The virtual order of social institutions

Parsons saw 'structure', in its most general sense, as referring to 'a set of relatively stable patterned relationships of units', and he concluded that a specifically 'social structure' is 'a patterned system of social relationships of actors' (Parsons 1945a: 230, 1975: 103). These patterns of social relations are to be understood, he argued, as normative patterns – as social institutions.

A major influence on Parsons's work was the early 'institution-alist' writings in economic sociology undertaken by Veblen (1899, 1904) and Commons (1899–1900; 1924). Commons defined social institutions as the 'definite and accepted modes of mutual dealing' that prevail in a society (Commons 1899–1900: 3). They are expressed in common usages, customs, and laws that shape individual desires and actions. The forms of action studied by economists and political scientists – actions in the market place and in electoral competition – are grounded in specifically economic and political institutions, and these, in turn, are grounded in the more general social institutions studied by sociology. Commons's argument on this point unwittingly echoed Durkheim's (1893) recognition of the 'non-contractual element in contract', the normative framework of trust and obligation that is presupposed by any contractual relationship. Parsons felt that the institutional economists tended to overstate the extent to which institutions were grounded in 'instincts', and he drew on Durkheim to build a specifically sociological approach to the formation of social institutions, as well as the ideas of the Boas school of cultural analysis.

Social institutions, for Parsons, constitute the framework or skeleton of a society. Examples include such large-scale structures as marriage, monogamy, endogamy, patriarchy, property, contract, collective bargaining, commodity exchange, bureaucracy, professionalism, sovereignty, representative government, monotheism, denominationalism, and selective education. There are, in addition, the micro-institutions of day-to-day existence, such as those concerned with queuing, turn taking in conversations, dinner party entertaining, and gift giving. These institutions, large-scale and micro, cluster together into overarching institutional structures such as feudalism, patrimonialism, industrialism, and capitalism.

These social institutions and institutional clusters must not be reified by the investigator. As cultural phenomena, they have a virtual and not a material existence:

> Institutional patterns are the 'backbone' of the social system. But they are by no means absolutely rigid entities and certainly have no mysteriously 'substantial' nature. They are only relatively stable

uniform resultants of the processes of behaviour of the members of the society.

(Parsons 1945b: 239)

Institutional patterns, therefore, are carried in the minds of individuals, but they have a virtual objectivity that puts them beyond particular individuals. Linton held that while the patterns 'are carried in the minds of individuals and can find overt expression only through the medium of individuals, the fact that they are shared by many members of a society gives them a super-individual character' (Linton 1936: 102). The institutional patterns persist while particular individuals come and go. An awareness of the subjective characteristics of social institutions must be tempered by an equal awareness of their objective reality.

Parsons himself has concentrated on the objective and external characteristics of social institutions, but a complementary account of the subjective origin of institutions was set out in the phenomenological work of Berger and Luckmann (1966; see also Holzner 1968). Social institutions, they argue, are built from the reciprocal expectations that people build up in their interactions. As someone observes another's actions, they infer meanings and motives and they begin to formulate these observations into enduring assumptions about what others will typically do in a variety of situations. These 'typifications' are, in Berger and Luckmann's words, 'inwardly appropriated' as normative expectations: actors infer that someone *will* typically act in such and such a way, and so they come to expect that they *ought* to act in that way. These expectations become objective and coercive social institutions when they are shared by participants and so come to be seen as self-evident, obvious, and taken-for-granted features of how the world really is. They become social facts that confront individuals and cannot be wished away (Berger and Luckmann 1966: 77). In many cases, of course, people are born into their social institutions. Rather than building them from scratch, they take them over ready formed, or they modify them only slightly. Individuals are socialized into their institutions as they are socialized into their culture.

Social institutions, then, have a dual reality, being both subjective and objective. As subjective realities, they are the 'maps' that people construct to guide themselves through their social interactions. Because individuals act on their knowledge, and because this knowledge is shared, social institutions become 'objectified'. They seem to the participants to have an objective reality outside themselves.

It is the interlocking of knowledge and actions among a plurality of individuals that gives social institutions their mind-independent characteristics. They are stable and rigid, and they cannot be altered by a simple individual refusal of them or a change of belief. They resist efforts to change them, and they constrain possibilities for action: 'If an insufficient number of people cease to believe in the reality of class, or racialism, or capitalism, then those few who start acting as though they did not exist will soon suffer a rude awakening' (Jarvie 1972: 150).

A structure of social institutions is not simply a construction in the individual mind; it is not reducible to the actual mental states of individuals. It is an objective, but non-substantial reality (Jarvie 1972: 152):

> On the one hand, social entities are, like mental states, intangible; like friendliness and goodwill they may come out of nothing and fade into nothing. On the other hand, they are like physical states, they react strongly to our probes: when, as an exercise, one *acts* as though a brick wall is not there, one may suffer severe consequences, and the same is true of many social institutions, from table manners to taxes.
>
> (Jarvie 1972: 159)

Social structure, then, is a conceptual reality whose elements are the culturally patterned expectations that are called social institutions. Social institutions are the 'normative patterns which define what are felt to be, in the given society, proper, legitimate or expected modes of action or of social relationship' (Parsons 1940b: 53, emphasis removed, 1960: 7–8). It is through institutions that practices become culturally standardized and actions are guided, regulated and channelled. They form 'predefined patterns of conduct, which channel it in one direction as against the many other directions that would theoretically be possible' (Berger and Luckmann 1966: 72). One of the clearest formulations of this point of view was that of Merton, who saw what he called the 'cultural structure' as 'that organized set of normative values governing behavior which is common to members of a designated society or group' (Merton 1957a: 162). The 'normative pattern' of a society comprises the regular and general ways of acting, thinking, and feeling that form people into social systems.

The idea of the 'normative pattern' shows that institutions are seen as built from 'norms'. A norm is seen, in its most general sense, as a rule of conduct that is shared by a particular set of people.

Norms do not set 'utopian' ideals for action, but are the actual, operative expectations that govern day-to-day behaviour. They define those things that people feel they have a right to expect of one another in specific circumstances. The basis of social order in everyday life is the sharing and interlocking of these behavioural expectations. As Davis has argued, 'The essence of any social situation lies in the mutual expectations of the participants' (Davis 1948: 83).[5] Any ongoing social situation involves a mutual recognition and sharing of behavioural expectations by the participants. Regularities in observed behaviour are brought about, to a greater or lesser extent, by the recognition of shared norms.

Many norms are acquired during socialization, through a process of internalization, and so there are great variations in the extent to which they are conscious and verbalized as clearly formulated principles of action. In some cases, people may be able to state them in some detail, while in others they will resort to vague generalities. They are very often taken-for-granted features of social life, and knowledge of them may be almost completely unconscious (Linton 1936: 259–60).

The explicit and written codifications of norms that are found in statutory law, handbooks of manners and etiquette, religious texts, and so on are not always the norms that people typically follow in their actual behaviour (Davis 1948: 70). People do not typically look in books in order to find out what they should do in everyday situations. Most of the time, people know what they must do without having to reflect on this for very long at all. People tend to become consciously aware of their norms when they are disregarded or challenged by others, or where they face novel and unfamiliar situations. In these situations, codified norms may be of particular significance. Codified rules of behaviour are also likely to be important as conscious principles for action whenever written legal norms are established by a conscious and deliberate act of authority. Legal norms are central to modern private property rights, citizenship rights, and to the control of certain forms of interpersonal violence, and many social institutions involve a mixture of legal and non-legal regulation. Norms can exist, therefore, both as internalized expectations and external codifications. Radcliffe-Brown rightly said that 'Rules . . . only exist in their recognition by the members of the society; either in their verbal recognition, when they are stated as rules, or in their observance in behaviour' (Radcliffe-Brown 1940: 198).

No matter how clear their knowledge of the particular norms regulating their own behaviour and that of those with whom they interact, few individuals will have any comprehensive and detailed knowledge of the overall structure of the social institutions of their society. They will have very little knowledge of the norms that are relevant to those who are distant from them or of how their own social positions are connected with all others into an extensive social division of labour. There is, then, a social distribution of knowledge: 'The patterns which comprise the system are transmitted to the individual as so many discrete units, and the knowledge and exercise of these patterns at any given point in the society's history is divided up among the society's members' (Linton 1936: 261). The knowledge that underpins the institutional structure is dispersed among the minds of the individuals who, through acting on their partial knowledge, reproduce – and transform – the objective and shared institutional structure that defines their various social positions and social expectations.

Institutions rediscovered

As we mentioned at the beginning of this chapter, structural functionalism faced many strident and persistent challenges during the 1960s and 1970s. This led many to abandon ideas of social institutions and institutional structure in favour of an emphasis on the irreducibility of individual action and face-to-face interaction found in 'micro-sociology' (see Chapter 6). All these approaches stressed the subjective reality of cultural phenomena – their location in individual minds – at the expense of their objective institutional reality. These concerns had a wider impact in the social sciences beyond sociology. Economics and political science had never been so deeply concerned with cultural issues, and in these disciplines an emphasis on individual action found its expression in particularly vociferous formulations of rational choice theory. During the 1980s, however, concern was growing over the limitations of these alternative perspectives and about what was being lost in a failure to take social institutions seriously. It was at this point that forms of 'neofunctionalism' began to appear in sociology, and variants of 'new institutionalism' were advocated in other social sciences.

Among economists, the new institutionalism involved a self-conscious rediscovery of the old institutionalism of Veblen and

Commons. It involved a recognition that rational economic actions, such as market transactions, are embedded in institutional frameworks that give them meaning and direction. New institutional economists see social institutions as providing the 'rules of the game', the procedures that give a sense of stability and orderliness to economic life and so reduce the uncertainty that people face in their day-to-day market transactions. These institutions provide the context within which economic transactions among enterprises and between enterprises and their customers take place.[6] They define and limit the range of choices that are open to people and so influence the outcome of market processes (North 1990: 3–4). The institutional framework of property rights, for example, forms a part of the structures of corporate governance that regulate the business behaviour of directors, executives, and managers. Writers such as Williamson (1981, 1985) saw institutions as the results of rational individual action and purposive design, while others saw them as the unintentional results of an evolutionary process of variation and selective retention (Nelson and Winter 1982). However they came about, they were recognized as a central aspect of any economic process (Granovetter 1986).

A similar perspective has been taken in political science about how social institutions regulate voting, decision making, and the formation of coalitions and alliances to exert pressure on governments. Much of this work has concentrated on formal administrative institutions, such as democracy, citizenship, and corporatism, and on such institutions as committee deliberation, budgeting, and judicial review. These institutions establish rules and procedures that regulate the distribution of authority, the generation and circulation of information, the allocation of time, the rights of opposition, and so on (March and Olsen 1989: 22). In a particularly famous example of this style of work, Bachrach and Baratz (1962) drew on the work of Schattschneider (1960) to show how the construction of political agendas and the establishment of procedures of decision making allows some groups to mobilize the institutional 'bias' and so exclude some people from power while advantaging others.

There has been a parallel development of new institutionalist writings in the interdisciplinary field of organization studies (Powell and DiMaggio 1991). This was pioneered by attempts to incorporate a more systematic awareness of the influence of culture on organizational forms, and this is the work that shows the greatest continuity with the work of the normative functionalists (Meyer and Rowan 1977; Meyer and Scott 1983; W. R. Scott 1995: 33).

Old institutionalism, normative functionalism, neofunctionalism, new institutionalism, and many other strands of thought have, then, jointly developed a concept of institutional structure as a cultural phenomenon that regulates social action. But how do they see this regulation as taking place, and what are its limits? The key mechanism of institutional regulation has been developed through the concepts of social positions and role expectations, and it is to these that we now turn.

Social positions and roles

Social institutions regulate actions by defining the social positions that people can occupy and the behaviour that is associated with these positions (Linton 1936). A social position is a definite 'social location' or 'social place' in a social system (Warner 1952: 46; Popitz 1967).[7] As a part of culture, knowledge about social positions is held in individual minds, but this knowledge is shared by those who interact together. Davis has remarked that

> An individual carries his social position around in his head, so to speak, and puts it into action when the appropriate occasion arises. Not only does he carry it in his head but others also carry it in theirs, because social positions are matters of reciprocal expectation and must be publicly and commonly perceived by everyone in the group.
>
> (Davis 1948: 87)

Social positions are elements in larger networks of positions. They are the units of the conceptual maps that people use to organize their social actions. Within these maps, they derive their specific meanings from their relations to other positions (Parsons 1942b: 143). Just as a particular word within a language derives its meaning from its relations to all other words (Saussure 1916), so social positions are defined relative to all the other social positions that comprise the social system in question. What it means to be a 'father', for example, depends upon how the culture defines what it is to be a 'child', a 'man', a 'husband', and so on. In their turn, each of these positions depends on what it is to be a father. Parsons concluded, therefore, that a social structure can be seen as 'a system of patterned relationships of actors in their capacity as playing roles relative to one another' (Parsons 1945a: 230).

The number of social positions that are identified in any particular culture is likely to be immense. Social institutions vary from one culture to another, and the social positions that they define will reflect this variability. Societies may distinguish, for example, such diverse positions as those of husband, wife, father, mother, neighbour, friend, headman, priest, doctor, citizen, dentist, plumber, church member, opera buff, and football fan. Even where a sociologist recognizes two cultures as each defining a social position of 'father', the way in which this position is seen and the name given to it may be quite different.

Each social position defines a role in social life for its occupants (Gross *et al.* 1958). Roles are definitions of those things that people are expected to do in the various situations that they encounter in their lives. They are blueprints or templates for action: 'bundles of expectations directed at the incumbents of positions in a given society' (Dahrendorf 1958: 36). They specify the rights and obligations that are entailed in social positions, and they tell us what is expected of us and what we should expect others to do (Parsons 1940b: 54). In this sense, roles specify the attitudes and behaviour that comprise the actual behaviour that occupants are expected to perform by providing people with a ready-made definition of the situation (Parsons 1942b: 145; Williams 1960: 35 ff.).[8]

Central to role expectations are ideas about *what* people should do and *how* they should do it. Merton has highlighted these two aspects of role expectations in his claim that the institutional structure of any society sets both the 'legitimate objectives' for social action and the 'regulatory norms' through which these objectives can legitimately be pursued (Merton 1949: 132). The objectives that are defined by a culture as being legitimate for particular individuals and groups to pursue are the goals, purposes, and interests that form the 'frame of aspiration' through which they live their lives. These objectives are held out to them as things to which they should aspire in their various social positions. The regulatory norms, on the other hand, define the acceptable means or avenues through which these objectives should be pursued. They proscribe certain forms of behaviour, they prescribe others, and they permit choice within specified limits.

Merton has argued that each social position is, in fact, associated with a whole array of forms of behaviour that comprise what he called a 'role set'. The audiences with whom a person interacts in his or her roles are, for the most part, the occupants of *different* positions, and so will have varying interests, sentiments, and values. A medical student, for example, must act as a student not only in relation to other students, but also in relation to clinical teachers, doctors, nurses, social workers, patients, medical technicians, and others. In each of these relations, the student is likely to encounter different behavioural expectations (Merton 1957b: 112). Clinical teachers may expect diligent study, supervising doctors may expect long hours of technically competent work, fellow students may expect sociability, and so on. Certain expectations may be shared by all role partners, though emphasized differently, while other expectations might differ quite markedly. Individuals must juggle the various expectations that make up their role set, as these may often conflict with one another. Satisfying the expectations of one participant may involve acting counter to the expectations of another. This has led to the recognition of varying degrees of 'role conflict', both within and between social roles.

Position and role always go together, and the distinction is, perhaps, a little artificial.[9] Nevertheless, the distinction between the location that a person occupies and the expectations that are attached to it is very important. This leads to the conclusion, in Parsons's words, that

> The institutional structure of a social system, then, is the totality of morally sanctioned statuses and roles which regulate the relations of persons to one another through 'locating' them in the structure and defining legitimate expectations of their attitude and behaviour.
> (Parsons 1942b: 143. He refers to the more general discussion in Parsons 1937: Chapters X and XV)

Conformity, power and contradictions

A major issue in institutional analysis is the question of why individuals conform to the normative expectations of their culture. For normative functionalists, conformity is seen as an inevitable consequence of a person's socialization into a cultural consensus. Fully socialized individuals internalize these cultural values during their early childhood and so the values become deeply embedded in the personality as 'moral sentiments'. People come to see conformity with institutionalized expectations as a moral duty, any violations of them being met with guilt or shame on the part of the violator and 'moral indignation' in their role partners. Guilt and indignation, then, are the 'corrective forces' that steer human behaviour (Parsons 1940b: 50; Williams 1960: 30, 31). The moral indignation of others can, of course, be expressed in many ways, varying from mild disapproval to the use of actual force.

Normative functionalists see the application of sanctions – rewards and punishments – as a supplementary source of social control. Where individuals have not been fully socialized, and so are more likely to deviate from the norms of their society, they may still conform in order to avoid the punishments or to obtain the rewards that this brings. These mechanisms of social control may even become organized into specialized social institutions: Parsons, for example, saw authority and status stratification as the most important institutional means through which sanctions are organized in a society (Parsons 1940a, 1940b).[10] Social institutions may, then, become associated with the 'vested interests' that individuals and groups acquire in them. Other things being equal, people are likely to seek to maintain the various benefits and advantages that they get from the way that the institutionalized patterns operate (Parsons 1942c: 139; 1945b: 241–2).

Despite this recognition that both moral sentiments and vested interests play a part in ensuring conformity to normative expectations, normative functionalists have justly been criticized for overemphasizing value consensus and for adopting an 'oversocialized' view of the individual (Wrong 1961). These critics have pointed out that the degree of consensus in a society may be quite low. In fact, normative functionalists have, themselves, always been unclear about how strongly the consensus assumption is to be taken. What seems to be clear is that the concept of institutional structure does not depend upon the strong assumption of complete consensus. While a particular society may rest on a common recognition of certain significant values and their associated norms, there need be no complete agreement over what particular value judgements and normative commitments are to be made. Fully socialized individuals may, for example, recognize the existence of property rights, but they need not subscribe to the moral legitimacy of these rights, and there may be all sorts of disputes about who enjoys particular rights in relation to specific objects.[11]

The existence of an institutional structure, then, does not require a complete moral consensus. This was actually recognized by Parsons, who said that 'when dynamic problems of directions and processes of change are at issue, it is essential to give specific attention to the elements of malintegration, tension and strain in the social structure' (Parsons 1942a: 117). That is to say, there can be incompatible or contradictory normative patterns within a culture, and particular individuals may experience all sorts of conflicting pressures upon them. In his discussion of German fascism, for example, Parsons showed that the institutional patterns of modern societies involve both 'traditional' and 'rationalized' elements and that these may generate conflicting demands or expectations (Parsons 1942c: 135). Merton quite explicitly said that the intensity of commitment to cultural objectives and norms is likely to vary from one group to another and that the same strong moral sentiments may not be shared by all members of a society (Merton 1957a: 170–2; Merton and Barber 1963).

This point was most explicitly recognized in the work of the conflict theorists, who argued that role expectations have to be seen in relation to the distribution of power (Dahrendorf 1958). A powerful social group may be able to impose its preferences on the less powerful by using its power to sanction nonconformity. In these circumstances, the institutions of a society will express the values of the powerful – who may not even form a majority. Any consensus that may exist will simply reflect the successful establishment of a dominant ideology (Rex 1961: 124–6). Shils (1961: 6) has also recognized that social institutions invariably involve a degree of imposition and that the actual or potential use of sanctions has to be seen as a normal feature of institutionalization. The central values that underpin the leading social institutions of a society, he argued, reflect the concerns of its dominant group, and tend to override the values and interests of more peripheral groups. Even Parsons recognized this possibility, holding that social institutions may simply comprise the '*dominant* structural outline' of a society (Parsons 1945b: 239).[12] Subordinate groups may have their own, quite distinct, norms and values, forming oppositional, 'anti-system' groups that pursue counter-institutions and become the agents of institutional change (Eisenstadt 1965: 41).

Power, then, may lead people to see conformity with normative expectations as necessary, even when they are not morally committed to them. Institutions can be accepted fatalistically or pragmatically, much as the weather is simply accepted because it is beyond our powers to change it (Mann 1970). The constraining force of social institutions, then, results from a combination of

value commitments and power and does not depend upon the existence of a moral consensus or even majority agreement (Dahrendorf 1958: 48). Thus, social structure is finally defined by Parsons as
'a system of patterned expectations defining the *proper* behaviour
of persons playing certain roles, enforced both by the incumbents'
own positive motives for conformity and by the sanctions of others'
(Parsons 1945a: 231).

A broadly similar understanding of the relationship between
institutional structure, power and conformity has been developed
by a number of theorists working in the Marxist tradition. As we
will show in Chapter 5, Marx did not reject the analysis of culture
and institutional structures, but he did not devote much attention
to delineating its relationship to the economic processes that he saw
as more fundamental. Institutional structure has, however, been
examined by later Marxist writers. The early members of the
Frankfurt school such as Horkheimer, Adorno, and Marcuse
looked at the role played by culture in the legitimation of capitalism. Their most influential works examined how the mass production of culture – the 'culture industry' – secured consent by turning
individuals into passive consumers of a 'debased' culture that
undermined their autonomy and stifled revolutionary protest.

A more powerful, and less pessimistic, account of institutional
structure was provided by Gramsci. He argued that national
societies and other social totalities should be seen as 'ensembles of
ideas and social relations' (Gramsci 1929–35: 366, 377), these social
relations being constituted by the crystallization of class forces and
the unequal distribution of economic resources. Gramsci maintained that classes could not rule by coercion alone, but also
required a cultural power – or 'hegemony' – through which the
active consent of the dominated could be secured. Cultural institutions formed a worldview, or 'common-sense' world, that organized and aligned the behaviour of individuals. Gramsci believed
that this institutional common sense was reproduced in the everyday activities of schools, churches, trade unions, and other organizations. This idea of institutional structure was developed by
Althusser (1971) in his concept of the 'ideological state apparatus'
(see also Williams 1977 and Dworkin 1997).

It is clear, then, that a recognition of the importance of patterns
of normative behaviour and the institutional structures that
underpin them is not incompatible with a recognition of the
importance of power and conflict. There can be no simplistic

equating of institutional analysis with a theory of consensus. Many institutional analysts have also made the point that there may be imbalances and inconsistencies between cultural elements, even where a high level of consensus does exist. Merton produced the most powerful example of this idea in his influential analysis of anomie.

Merton began from a recognition that the institutionalized objectives and regulatory norms that are attached to social positions do not always stand in a constant relation to one another. It is possible for the objectives and the means to be emphasized differently: 'The cultural emphasis placed upon certain goals varies independently of the degree of emphasis upon institutionalised means' (Merton 1949: 133). That is to say, in some societies the objectives are highly stressed, while the legitimacy of the means for attaining them is seen as being of less importance; in other societies exactly the opposite may hold, and the means may be stressed at the expense of the objectives. On this basis, Merton identified two extreme cases of social order, which he called the *anomic* and the *ritualistic* or fatalistic.[13] The anomic case is that where the objectives of actions are strongly emphasized and far less attention is given to the regulating norms. The opposite, fatalistic, case occurs where there is a strong emphasis on close adherence to prescribed ways of behaving, regardless of their actual results (Merton 1949). In his analysis, Merton concluded that US society was closer to the anomic form. Importantly this also led him to emphasize that the uneven access to legitimate means produced different forms of adaptation (conformist, innovative, ritualistic, retreatist and rebellious responses (Merton 1949: 139 ff.; Parsons 1951: 256–60)).[14]

Merton's argument highlights the fact that social structures should not be regarded as seamless and fully integrated. Ambivalence and incompatibility in institutional patterns is inherent in social structure. Lockwood (1964) has usefully described the incompatibilities between social institutions and their elements as aspects of 'system integration', with significant incompatibilities creating 'system contradictions'. In Lockwood's terms, system contradictions exist when there are incompatibilities between the patterns or principles around which particular institutions or clusters of institutions are organized. In the words of Mouzelis:

> The concept of system contradiction means that principles of organis-
> ation dominant in a certain institutional sphere are more or less

incompatible with the organising principles operating in other institutional spheres of the same social system.

(Mouzelis 1991: 60)

A celebrated – perhaps notorious – example of such a system
contradiction is Parsons's claim that there is an incompatibility
between the norms around which the extended family is organized
(particularism and emotional attachement) and the central norms
of an industrial economy (universalism and value neutrality).
Another example might be the Marxian argument that system contradictions between technological institutions (forces of production) and property institutions (relations of production) are the
driving force in social change.

The use of institutional analysis can be illustrated from two
examples. Our point in giving these examples is not to claim that
these particular uses of institutional concepts give correct descrip-
tions of the world – though they both have a degree of empirical
support. Rather, our aim is to show how the concepts can be used
in concrete sociological work. The first case that we will look at is
the analysis of medical practice. The second is the exploration of
kinship, marriage, and patriarchy.

The case of medical practice

The centrepiece of Parsons's book *The Social System* (Parsons
1951) is, in many ways, his analysis of doctor–patient relations as a
role system defined by the social institutions of health care and professionalism. He saw the position of the doctor as that of a trained
medical expert, a position in the modern occupational division of
labour. The ill person, however, also takes on a social position, and
Parsons described this as the 'sick role'. When the ill person is
under professional medical treatment, the sick role becomes the
role of the patient. From this point of view, then, illness is not
simply a biological condition, it is an institutionalized social role
and a 'career'.

Social institutions of professional health care are specific to the
modern world, where they are underpinned by the cultural tradition of modern science that gives them meaning. Modern science
defines the importance of bodily health and of the technically
appropriate therapies that are aimed at maintaining or restoring
health (Parsons 1951: 432). Care for the sick remains an element in

certain domestic roles (most particularly those of the mother and of other female kin), but it has increasingly been differentiated into specialized occupations, such as that of the doctor. These occupations are organized, in part, through the social institution of scientific, clinical medicine. The autonomy of the expert practitioners within specialized agencies, such as clinics and hospitals, are geared to health care and, as Foucault (1963) argued, they are organized around particular cultural forms of discourse that define conceptions of normality and deviance.

Doctors are expected to have a high level of technical competence and skill, based on their expert knowledge, and they are recruited from among those who have undergone a lengthy and intense period of training. Their occupation is regulated by norms of professionalism that provide them with a code of practice that limits their pursuit of economic self-interest and sets them apart from those occupations that are regulated mainly by business and commercial institutions. Parsons held that the institution of professionalism involves the normative patterns of universalism, neutrality, performance, and specificity that characterize all the technical occupational roles of modern society. These occupational roles make up the institutional division of labour in a society. However, professionalism combines these with normative orientations that limit the expression of self-interested motivations and allow the adoption of a disinterested, 'service' orientation towards those who are designated as sick.

A service orientation means that the doctor is expected to put the well-being of the patient above his or her own personal interests. Where medicine is organized along the lines of private provision, rather than state provision, considerations of income and profit are held to be secondary to the commitment to improving the health of the patient, and the medical profession is organized around the use of sanctions to maintain this (Parsons 1951: 435–6). The doctor cannot advertise – except with a modest brass plate and an entry in a telephone directory – and he or she can adjust charges according to the perceived 'need' or income of the patient. The service professional cannot offer discounts or special deals for medical treatment. Conversely, the patient is expected to place trust in the expertise of the doctor and not to shop around for better – or different – treatment.

The person who feels ill, and is known to feel ill, also faces a definite set of expectations that define a 'sick role' for them to play.

When properly accredited as an incumbent of the sick role – for example, when recognized as 'ill' by those with the expertise and authority to do so – the sick person is permitted to withdraw from many of the normal obligations attached to his or her other social positions. The sick role gives dispensation from some normal obligations. The sick person also, however, acquires new obligations: most notably, the obligation to 'get well' again by cooperating with the medical treatment that is offered by the doctor (Parsons 1951: 436–8). The doctor–patient relationship is supposed to be one of cooperation and trust, and this is the basis of the doctor's authority: the patient is supposed to accept 'doctor's orders' as valid and legitimate. Getting better means abandoning the sick role and gradually taking on again all the obligations that are attached to a person's normal social positions.

Foucault has shown that all forms of discursive knowledge involve relations of power to sustain them and make them effective. The exercise of medical control over the body is, he argued, an 'anatomo politics' that not only regulates but disciplines (Foucault 1976). Individuals are culturally formed as self-disciplining bodies, and whole populations establish regimes of fertility and vitality. Foucault's recognition of power relations, however, highlights the partial and one-sided character of a purely institutional account of medicine. The essential insights of institutional analysis must be complemented by a focus on the relational structures with which they are involved.

The case of kinship and marriage

Murdock's influential statement (1949) saw kinship and marriage as the social institutions that regulate the consanguinity and affinity of individuals. Consanguinity is a term that refers to the culturally assumed blood relationships of descent and parentage. Kinship institutions are those that are specifically concerned with defining and regulating the relations of descent that result from whatever blood relations are recognized by the members of a society. By contrast with biological or ecological approaches to descent, sociology and anthropology are concerned only with those relations that are culturally *recognized* as blood relations. The biological reality of these relations is of secondary importance, as Radcliffe-Brown recognized: 'Kinship . . . results from the recognition of a social relationship between parents and children, which is not the same thing as the physical relation, and may not coincide with it' (Radcliffe-Brown 1950: 4). Kinship is likely to be associated with other more specialized social institutions that modify its effects. The institution of adoption, through which those without an assumed biological relationship are treated as if they were blood relatives, for example, allows those who are not consanguines to be incorporated into a kinship group.

Affinity is a general term for the combination of people into social and domestic units. Marriage, whether legal or customary, is the social institution that defines the legitimate forms of affinity for a society, regulating sexual cohabitation (through the establishment of compulsory heterosexuality and through restrictions on incest and homosexual pairing) and economic cooperation. Because it defines the legitimate conditions of human reproduction, it also tends to specify patterns of care and socialization. Related institutions of divorce and domestic service help to define further the specific character of marriage in a society.

Jointly, these social institutions can define large numbers of kinship positions, each being defined relative to the other kinship positions that make up a kinship system. The result is sets of 'relatives': 'Every kinship system provides each person in a society with a set of dyadic (person to person) relationships, so that he stands, as it were, at the centre of a narrower or wider circle of relatives' (Radcliffe-Brown 1950: 39).

Cultures vary in the particular positions that they identify and in the terminology that they adopt to describe them. Although it may be impossible to translate the categories of one culture directly into those of another, the positions most typically found in systems of kinship and marriage include those of parent and child, grandparent and grandchild, aunt/uncle and nephew/niece, husband and wife, siblings, and cousins. Distinctions may be made between maternal and paternal relatives, hence identifying those who are 'in-laws'. The application of kinship, marriage, adoption, and other institutions and norms allows an even larger and more complex set of relatives to be identified.

Kinship and marriage define the expectations of behaviour that are thought to be appropriate to those in each position that has been institutionalized. These may establish obligations of affection, care, and cooperation, rights to authority within a domestic unit, preferential marital patterns, and so on. Such definitions are also closely associated with culturally recognized differences of gender, the main kinship positions being gender-specific and associated with prevailing norms of masculinity and femininity. Norms of residence, legitimacy, inheritance of property, names, and titles, and succession to authority may also be involved, and these can coexist in various ways. Murdock has suggested that while matrilineal descent, matrilineal inheritance, and matrilocal residence are frequently found together, it is possible for them to occur independently of each other: matrilineal descent may, for example, be combined with patrilocal residence and patrilineal inheritance (Murdock 1949: 37–8).

Weber (1914) saw the domestic institution of patriarchalism as existing when kinship and marriage norms establish the authority of the father over a whole household. This is a form of 'traditional authority' in which the legitimacy of the father's power is traced back through the male line to the original formation of the household or to time immemorial. The institutional structure of patriarchalism gives the father absolute personal power over the life fates of those in his household (Barrett 1980; Hamilton 1984; Sydie 1987. See also Engels 1884).

Weber saw patriarchalism as one of the key institutional elements in the larger institutional structures of patrimonialism and feudalism, but feminist writers have generalized the idea even more widely in the form of 'patriarchy'. The institution of patriarchy is most typically seen as defining differences of power and advantage between men and women, and it is seen as a universal – or near-universal – feature of human society. It is the institutional definition of male dominance over women, which has its roots in the institutions of marriage and kinship (Delphy 1977). As such, it is not simply a domestic or familial institution, but a general normative pattern that organizes social life in a whole range of social settings. Patriarchy defines generalized male dominance: men as a category dominate women as a category (Millet 1970; Hartsock 1984; Murray 1995).

Transnational and post-colonial challenges

Recently an important strand of sociological theory has questioned the equation of the ideas of 'society' and the nation state that much institutional analysis has assumed. It has been argued that societies existed before the development of the nation state, and that, even in nation states, social structures need not be seen as operating exclusively within its confines. Mann (1986: 377), for example, has shown that Christendom provided a regulative 'ideological network', or institutional structure, that integrated the otherwise divided political units of medieval Europe. Similarly, Robertson has shown that international trade and commerce presupposed the existence of transnationally valid cultural norms (see also Woodiwiss 1998).

It is certainly the case that the institutional analyses discussed in this chapter have tended to see institutional structures within the contexts of national cultures and societies. Nevertheless, it is also true that Parsons, most notably in his evolutionary work, framed his analysis of the development of cultural systems at the level of the world system (Parsons 1971b). In principle, then, the concept of institutional structure is compatible with a transnational perspective. Indeed, in the next chapter we will show that it has been combined with the concept of relational structure to describe social relations at the subnational level of the city and the transnational level of the world system.

A related, but different, challenge to institutional analysis has come from post-colonial and cultural studies, where the 'Eurocentrism' of much western theorizing has been questioned. Ideas about western historical development and the representation of the 'other', it has been argued, must take account of the power of exclusion and the pathologization of other cultures that this presupposes (Said 1978. See also Grossberg *et al.* 1992; During 1993; Tiffin and Lawson 1994; McClintock *et al.* 1997). The claim that institutional structures must be seen in the context of the distribution of power, however, is a point that we have already stressed and that we will continue to develop in later chapters. Indeed, many of these critical texts imply that the concept of institutional structure should be further developed, and not abandoned, precisely in order to engage with these pressing questions.[15]

A further challenge from cultural and post-colonial studies has been strengthened by the post-modern critique of social theory. This is the challenge to the assumption of cultural homogeneity that models of institutional structure seem to presuppose. It is argued that institutional analysis cannot handle cultural and institutional heterogeneity or the ways in which differently positioned groups resist the imposition of hegemonic, cultural categories and struggle to articulate oppositional identities. In exploring the development of the concept of institutional structure we have argued that, though not entirely absent, diversity and struggle for cultural recognition have, indeed, not received sufficient attention. In Chapters 5 and 6 we return to these questions by looking at ways in which ideas of heterogeneity can be reconciled with conceptions of both institutional and relational structures. Nonetheless, it is worth emphasizing that, despite the existence of cultural diversity, it is nevertheless the case that much of social life is characterized by the kind of cultural homogeneity that makes the idea of institutional structure viable.

In this chapter, we have concentrated on the key ideas of institutional analysis, exploring the cultural definition of the positions and roles that are the basis of the normative regulation of individual and collective action. However, there is more to social action than normative regulation. Social structure, we argued in Chapter 2, comprises both institutional structure and relational structure, and neither of these can be simply derived from the other. This is clear from our illustrative discussion of patriarchy. In much feminist writing it is stressed that patterns of patriarchy are not purely institutional in character. Individual behaviour, as we have seen, is not the result of perfect socialization into cultural norms, and clusters of social institutions involve many inconsistencies and incompatibilities. A full consideration of the social structure of patriarchy – as of any social structure – requires an analysis of relational structure as well as institutional structure. It is to a consideration of relational structure that we will turn to in the next chapter.

4
Relational Structure

In Chapter 3 we looked at the ways in which the normative aspects of social structure have been explored, and we have shown that many approaches to institutional analysis have treated relational structure as being of secondary or derivative importance. There has been a tendency to assume the perfect institutionalization of social relations through consensus and socialization, leaving no apparent need to engage in any separate analysis of social relations.

Our discussion of the institutional approach to kinship, marriage and patriarchy highlighted the inadequacy of this assumption. While feminist writers have pointed to the institutional underpinning of patriarchy through customary and traditional norms of marriage, inheritance, and femininity, many have also stressed that patriarchal power goes beyond the normative structuring of action to set distinct relational constraints on the actions of men and women. Thus, Barrett (1988) concluded that it is useful to employ the idea of patriarchy to grasp the non-institutional, as well as the institutional, aspects of women's oppression by men. This argument has been developed in a particularly powerful and important way by Walby (1990), who recognized relational structures of patriarchy as being fundamental to the organization of male/female social relations in a range of social situations: domestic divisions of labour, occupational segregation in labour markets, female exclusion and marginalization in the state, and relations of male violence against women. These are not normatively sanctioned and legitimated social institutions. The 'glass ceiling' that blocks women from entering the top levels of the state, for example, is not a legitimizsed feature of institutional role expectations, though it does depend upon the existence of institutionalized gender roles.

The case for a relational understanding of social organization was also a crucial plank in Marx's critique of German idealism. The crisp summary in the *Theses on Feuerbach* (Marx 1845) held that social life had to be understood as an 'ensemble' of social relations. Combined with his emphasis on productive practices, this point of view allowed Marx to develop an account of social organization as based, ultimately, on the unequal distribution of economic resources. Thus, the possession of the means of production by a capitalist class presupposes the existence of a proletariat class that is forced to sell its labour in order to survive. This understanding of social relations as constituted, in part, through access to, and control over, different types of resources is a recurrent theme in approaches to relational structure.

In this chapter, we look at the ideas of those who have attempted to understand relational structure without reducing it to institutional structure. We will look, in particular, at the arguments of British social anthropologists influenced by Radcliffe-Brown and the German formal sociologists who sought to develop a systematic analysis of social relations. These two strands of thought led to powerful conceptions of relational structure, especially in the hands of the so-called conflict theorists. We will show how they also generated the central ideas of social network analysis, which has rapidly advanced as a way of furthering these conceptual claims.

Relational structure in anthropology

Radcliffe-Brown and his fellow social anthropologists, as we showed in Chapter 3, contributed a great deal to the understanding of institutional structure, seeing actual social relations as shaped by the norms into which people are socialized. Many of those that they influenced took a very one-sided view of this. They looked only at those fully institutionalized relationships where social relations correspond exactly to the norms that generate them in a one-to-one way. This tendency to focus on the limiting case of the perfectly institutionalized social relation, the social relation that corresponds exactly to the normative pattern, became a prominent theme in the sociology of the postwar period (see Fletcher 1965; Wells 1970). Even the most committed normative functionalist, however, recognized that socialization and moral commitment are never perfect and that actual social relations do tend to depart from the normatively preferred pattern. While Parsons and his school gave relatively little attention to social relations as phenomena in their own right, Radcliffe-Brown did provide a way forward for those who wished it. His ideas have had a lasting influence on the work of those who have sought to understand relational structure.

Radcliffe-Brown's account of the Andaman islanders (Radcliffe-Brown 1922) was thoroughly Durkheimian in character, and to its structural ideas he added a keen insight into human psychology that he had derived from Rivers (1906, 1924) and McDougall (McDougall 1908), his teachers and colleagues at Cambridge. His central contention was that the social relations of a society depend on the existence and maintenance of a system of sentiments or emotional tendencies. These sentiments – what Durkheim called the *conscience collective* – exist in the minds of the individual members of the society and are transmitted from generation to generation through religious ceremonies and rituals (Durkheim 1912). Both social relations and shared sentiments had to be studied through scientific methods, Radcliffe-Brown held, and he set out these methods in a set of lectures at Chicago University, later published as *A Natural Science of Society* (Radcliffe-Brown 1937).

A natural science, Radcliffe-Brown argued, strives to explain the observed relations between particular events (1937: 6). It typically does so through causal laws that describe the interconnections in space and time through which things are formed into 'systems'. A system is an organized whole, a set of interconnected elements, that exists within a surrounding environment from which it is, nevertheless, distinct (ibid. 14–15, 19). It is the pattern of interconnections among the elements that gives it a definite structure. As examples of natural systems, Radcliffe-Brown cited physical objects, biological organisms, human minds and, of course, societies. Each of these systems is the object of a separate science. Where chemistry investigates the molecular structures of substances and anatomy investigates the biological structures of organisms, sociology investigates the social structures of human societies.

Like Durkheim, Radcliffe-Brown saw the science of society – sociology – as distinct from the science of individual mental states. Psychology is the science of mind, and mind is the particular system that is formed when the acts of an individual are interconnected through subjective mental relations. 'Society', on the other hand, is the system that is formed when the acts of different individuals are connected through social relations (ibid.: 43–4). A social system is a system of individual human beings who are involved in social relations with each other (ibid.: 43).

Human action, Radcliffe-Brown held, is purposive and interested, and a social relation exists among two or more individuals when there is a mutual adaptation, or 'coaptation', of their interests. Coaptation involves a modification of behaviour in relation to the assumed intentions of others, and so any social relation must involve some kind of communication or 'exchange of ideas' (ibid.: 47) between the minds of the participants. As more and more social relations are built, so the separate individuals become 'connected by a complex network of social relations'. It is this 'network of actually existing relations' that Radcliffe-Brown called the 'social structure' of a society. Social structure, then, is 'the sum total of all the social relationships of all individuals at a given moment in time' (Radcliffe-Brown 1940: 190, 55).

Radcliffe-Brown makes it clear, however, that a social structure is not simply the concrete pattern of interconnections that can be immediately observed. Just as the structure of a building is something other than the actual physical arrangement of its bricks, one on top of another, so a social structure is something other than the flux of interconnections that can be found through casual observation. The particular and unique connections that exist among specific people at any given moment in time are simply the raw materials from which it may be possible to infer the existence of social relations proper. Observation of behaviour in domestic settings, for example, may suggest certain similarities in the acts of men towards particular children and of children towards particular men. From these observations, the existence of a specific social relation – that of father to child – may be inferred. Radcliffe-Brown held that 'The actual relations of Tom, Dick and Harry or the behaviour of Jack and Jill' (Radcliffe-Brown 1940: 192) are the contingent raw materials from which we infer the general and enduring relations of father to child, husband to wife, brother to sister, and so on. This inference is guided by the knowledge of the sociological observer, and it is what allows us to move from concrete observations to the investigation of social structures.

Social relations are general and recurrent within a society. It is this generality that gives a common 'structural form' (Radcliffe-Brown 1937: 55) to a social relation wherever it appears in the society. The structural form of a social relation is the 'general or normal form' that lies behind 'the variations of particular instances'

(Radcliffe-Brown 1940: 192).[1] A generalized structural form of 'the family', for example, lies behind the specific instances of the López, Scott, or Radcliffe-Brown families. It is this generality that makes the structural form a social fact.

Radcliffe-Brown's position was enlarged upon by Nadel (1951), who explicitly distinguished the study of relational 'groupings' from the study of normative 'institutions'.[2] A grouping or association is 'a collection of individuals who stand in regular and relatively permanent relationships, that is, who act towards and in respect of each other, or towards and in respect of individuals outside the group, regularly in a specific, predictable, and expected fashion' (Nadel 1951: 146). Through this idea of the relational grouping, Nadel moved towards the analysis of larger configurations of relations than those instanced by Radcliffe-Brown. People are likely to be conscious of their membership in these groupings and so will tend to build up bonds of obligation and responsibility that may become institutionalized norms of behaviour. Nadel's key point, however, was that groupings could not be reduced to institutions, and *vice versa*: relational structure and institutional structure were separate and interdependent aspects of structural explanation.

While the distinction between relations and norms is not, to be sure, an absolute one, it is nevertheless fundamental. Social relations exist only by virtue of the norms or rules that people apply in their actions, but the relations cannot simply be read-off from the rules. There is no necessary one-to-one relationship between the two. A failure to work through the implications of this fundamental point has been responsible for a persistent confusion between social relations and social institutions. In the work of Malinowski and many later writers, the distinction between these two was not always retained, and they have often been conflated as they were in the works of the normative functionalists. As a result, the importance of the actual social relations has tended to be minimized, and social structure has been seen simply as a system of institutions. Even Radcliffe-Brown sometimes slipped into seeing social structure as 'any arrangement of persons in institutionalized relationships' (Radcliffe-Brown 1950: 43). Nevertheless, he saw a principal task for structural analysis as being the description of the actual social relations in which people are involved and the structural forms that these exhibit. Once this task has been carried out, he held, it is possible to investigate the normative patterns that might be responsible for the relational patterns. Each task can be properly undertaken only if their distinctiveness is kept clearly in mind.

The ideas of Radcliffe-Brown and Nadel encouraged many sociologists and anthropologists to investigate relational structures more directly, and it was through this work that the idea of the relational structure as a 'social network' began to develop. A major inspiration behind this idea of the social network, however, was the parallel work of sociologists in Germany who developed what has come to be called formal sociology.

Social structure as relational forms

The figure most closely associated with the idea of a formal, relational sociology is Simmel, whose ideas had a major impact on the attempts by Tönnies and Weber to construct foundational concepts for historical and comparative studies and were the major inspiration behind the more explicitly conceptual works of Vierkandt (1923) and von Wiese. This relational approach dominated German sociology from the 1890s through to the Nazi rise to power in the 1930s. Simmel's sociology also had a direct impact on sociology in the United States through Albion Small's many translations from his work. Together with the adaptation and enlargement of von Wiese's work in the hands of Howard P. Becker (Wiese–Becker 1932) and the ideas learned by the many American sociologists who undertook doctoral studies in Germany, relational sociology became a major influence on the developing work of the Chicago sociologists. At about the same time, Karl Mannheim, an emigré from Nazi Germany, was lecturing on systematic sociology, presenting very similar ideas to a British audience (Mannheim 1934–5). The final expression of this approach in classical German sociology itself, published on the eve of the Second World War, was the work of Mannheim's assistant, Norbert Elias (1939), but his work was virtually ignored until the 1960s and was not at all well known outside Germany until he drew out its more systematic aspects (Elias 1969).

Simmel's early work on stratification (1890), money (1900), and religion (1906) led him to move towards the more strictly relational sociology that he developed in a series of essays written in the 1890s and early 1900s. These essays were brought together as a systematic treatise in his *Sociology* (Simmel 1908).[3] Simmel rejected any approach to social life that seemed to accord a substantial existence to society itself. He held that society is not a substance in itself, but is manifested in the dynamic relations that exist among individuals. Society is not a thing, but a process. From this point of view, the shared ideas and collective representations that exist in individual minds and that comprise the *content* of social life and the motivations for actions must be seen as expressed externally in objective *forms* of social relationship. Actions with economic or educational goals, for example, may be equally 'competitive', and the nature or form of the competition can be analysed quite independently of the particular contexts in which it occurs.

Simmel sought to identify what he called the 'forms of sociation' (*Vergesellschaftung*) or solidarity that occur in a wide variety of cultural contexts and that can, therefore, be analysed independently of the specific 'content' that they have in these contexts. The method of sociology involves abstracting the pure forms of social life from their various historical contents, much as the method of geometry involves abstracting the form of the circle from particular round objects and the form of the triangle from particular three-sided objects. Simmel recognized, however, that no absolute separation of form from content was possible. Many of the actual concepts that he set out in his formal sociology do not describe simply the abstract 'geometrical' forms of social life, but are defined also by specific kinds of content, such as the particular purposes, interests, or desires that motivate them.

This methodological analogy with mathematics and the natural sciences was also explored by Tönnies, whose *Community and Association* (1889) was followed by the ventures into systematic, relational sociology that he undertook during the 1920s and 1930s. Scientific concepts, he argued, are not concrete realities; they are abstract constructions of thought. Science deals with such abstractions as the extensionless point, the straight line, the vacuum, and so on. Sociology has to proceed in the same way by constructing what Tönnies called 'normal concepts'. These never, or very rarely, appear in their pure form in any of their concrete occurrences. Social forms are always mixed and entangled with each other, as they are with physical and mental phenomena.

There was also a continuity between Simmel's and Weber's methodological work. Weber's essay (1904) on the ideal type can be read as an expansion of Simmel's idea of the pure form, though Weber initially narrowed this down to the particular, historically circumscribed phenomena that he called 'historical individuals'. In

other works, however, he recognized a variety of types of social
action in much the same way as Simmel had done (Weber 1920).
Simmel himself increasingly wrote of the 'type' (*Typus* or *Art*)
rather than the 'form' (*Form*) – indeed, he sometimes described this
as the 'form type' (*Formtypus*), just as Weber had described his
concept as the ideal type (*Idealtypus*).

Simmel's forms of sociation, then, aimed to describe patterns of
action in a pure and abstract way, separately from their concrete
historical realizations. Any social action is likely to combine
together a number of different forms of relation, which may not be
completely compatible with each other. The relation between a
buyer and a seller of a commodity, for example, can involve both
competition and coercion, as well as persuasion, secrecy, and
inequality. 'A multitude of forms are present in every social situation as a historical phenomenon, and each limits the realization of
the other. Consequently, only "distorted" forms can be discovered
in reality' (Tenbruck 1959: 79). The forms are identified only by
taking these distorted versions and exaggerating certain of their
characteristics until they can be identified in a purely one-sided
manner. In this way, the sociologist is 'selecting and exaggerating
features of . . . reality in order to bring out the inherent, structural
order of the elements involved' (Tenbruck 1959: 79).

How, then, are these social forms understood by Simmel? They
are not to be understood, he said, as ideas or representations in
people's minds. They are, rather, actual relations among individuals
that show a reciprocal effect, interdependence, or interweaving
(*Wechselswirkung*) of actions. In much the same way, Weber (1920)
saw a social relation as existing wherever there is a 'mutual adjustment' in the behaviour of two or more individuals, who thereby
converge on a persistent and regular pattern of joint behaviour.
Relations are defined by the likelihood that the people involved
will act in certain predictable ways, whatever the basis (or content)
on which this occurs. Only if there is an actual likelihood of definite patterns of meaningful social action occurring, can it be said
that a social relation exists or endures. The social process comprises
the interweaving of actions into more or less complex patterns. The
individual, therefore, is merely 'the point at which the social
threads entwine themselves' (Simmel 1908: 2).[4]

'Interweaving' was one of Simmel's key ideas. Metaphors of tex-
tiles and threads abounded in classical German sociology as a way
of exploring social relations. Von Wiese used an analogy with the

carpet. A carpet is woven from numerous multicoloured threads and, despite the diversity of these threads, the carpet shows a definite pattern. In the same way, the historical process can be seen as the outcome of innumerable individual actions, forming patterns that are situated and develop outside any one individual. These forms of relation, then, are both general and external. They comprise an 'external network' that has regularities of its own. Echoing Simmel's textile metaphors, Elias later argued that the 'social web' is to be seen as a substratum within which individuals spin and weave their actions. People are interdependent elements within 'figurations' of interweaving actions or networks of interdependencies (Elias 1969: 21, 12).

What are often called social structures, Simmel argued, are simply 'crystallizations' of simpler social relations. Simmel variously refers to these crystallizations as constellations, configurations, and concatenations, but only rarely as 'structures'.[5] They include states, economies, classes, divisions of labour, and many other large-scale social structures, but they also include the minor face-to-face interactions from which these major formations are built. These 'trifling threads' sustain the larger structures and prevent societies from fragmenting into a 'multitude of discontinuous systems' (Simmel 1908: 15).

Simmel's structural sociology (1908) used size and space as fundamental organizing principles for discussing relations of power and conflict. He showed, for example, that speculations about the differences between the political and the religious characteristics of small and large groups could be substantially refined by using more precise measures of 'small' and 'large'. To this end, he constructed a conceptual framework that began from the isolated individual and moved through the dyad and the triad to larger groups, showing how the opportunities for participants vary in each case. The individual actor, for example, exists as an individual because of his or her isolation from others. Simmel saw this, however, not as the absence of society but as a rejection of or exclusion from it. Isolation is, therefore, a social relation, and its effects can be studied through investigating strangers, pariahs, and other outsiders in otherwise cohesive communities or social gatherings.

When a dyad[6] exists, new forms of relation become possible for the participants: the members of a dyad can, for example, achieve varying degrees of intimacy and can share secrets that tie them together and give them a common fate. Each participant in a dyad feels that he or she is confronted by a specific other, even though the two are seen as a unit by outsiders. The addition of a third member to such a group creates the possibility for coalitions of two actors against the third, for jealousy, and for new forms of power. One of the three participants, for example, may be able to act as an intermediary between the other two and so gain numerous advantages from a prominence in the control of information and resources. As groups increase in size, Simmel argued, so the possibility of a stable and secure 'super-personal' sphere of life becomes possible. Complex configurations of relations such as states and churches acquire a solidity and reality that it is not possible for smaller groups to achieve.

Simmel was not a systematic writer, preferring to use the essay form to develop his ideas on specific topics. Despite bringing many of his essays together into a single volume, he was himself dissatisfied by the inconsistencies that he saw in his work. Levine (1991) has suggested that a more systematic reconstruction of what Simmel was doing would have required an extended discussion of such issues as inequality, antagonism, and assimilation alongside the discussion of size, and this was, in fact, attempted by Mannheim (1934–5). Despite this lack of systematization – or, paradoxically, it may have been because of it – Simmel had a substantial impact on the development of relational ideas. Weber (1920), for example, looked at conflict, competition, and social selection and at the ways in which these vary in open or closed, communal or rational relations. Weber used these general features of social relations to build concepts of household, market, estate, class, church, and state. What he called social formations (*soziale Gebilde*) are seen as resulting from the connections created among particular individuals in their social relations. Similarly, Tönnies looked at dyadic social relations and at how they can concatenate into extended social circles, clusters, or cliques of social relations that may, in turn, be formed into various kinds of 'configurations' or 'entities'. The most important of these are what Tönnies called 'collectivities' and 'corporations'. These are relatively unified forms of social action that are capable of acting in concert. Collectivities include such things as teams, classes, and nations, while corporations include business enterprises, churches, and states. In a corporation, there is a more or less clear constitution and an awareness on the part of the participants that they are 'members' of this larger body (Tönnies 1931: 143 ff.). Tönnies constructed an array of concepts to

describe particular types of social relations, collectivities, and corporations: these included domination, fellowship, union, association, league, class, estate, party, family, nation, guild, church, state,
and more abstract relational entities such as systems of religion.
These relational formations (*Bezugsgebilde*) are not understood as
involving institutionalized role relationships, though many of them
will, of course, do so. They are, rather, relations of causal interdependence in social actions that result from particular types of
motivation.

The most systematic follower of Simmel's approach to social
relations was von Wiese, whose work was developed in conjunction
with Becker (Wiese–Becker 1932) and was very influential in the
United States. These writers sought to take the geometrical
approach to social life as far as they could, seeing social relations
in terms of such variables as 'direction', 'intensity', and 'distance'.

The two directions that social relations could take Wiese and
Becker called 'association' and 'dissociation'. Positive relations of
association involve reciprocity, approach, or harmony, while negative relations of dissociation involve hostility, avoidance, or conflict.
Each type of relation varies not only in its intensity, but also in
terms of the distance between the participants. Thus, people may
be moving towards or away from each other over greater or lesser
social distances, though social distances are 'sometimes but not
always spatially evident' (Wiese–Becker 1932: 154). Social life is a
mesh of interpersonal connecting lines, and the task of sociology is
to trace the 'web' or 'network' that is woven by relations of association and dissociation (pp. 52, 68). This has great similarities with
the concept of social space that was being developed by Sorokin
(1927) and in the 'sociometry' of Moreno (1934). From this point
of view, the location of a person is defined by his or her relations to
other people, and the totality of these relations provides a system
of coordinates for defining and locating any person in a social space
or social structure. The basic sociological frame of reference, then,
describes movements of convergence and divergence among
human beings in social space.

Von Wiese and Becker's sociometry required a comprehensive
classification of social relations, and they developed this at great
length, producing a scheme of some hundreds of types of social
relations. Relations of association, they argued, take a great variety
of concrete forms, which they classified into the ten categories of
advance, adjustment, accordance, amalgamation, uniformation,

super- and subordination, socialization, institutionalization, profes-
sionalization, and liberation. Similarly, they classified relations
of dissociation into the thirteen categories of competition, con-
ravention, conflict, domination, gradation, selection, separation,
exploitation, favouritism, formalization, commercialization, radi-
calization, and perversion (Wiese-Becker 1932: 717 ff.).[7] In exploring how these relations connect together, they examined such social
forms as hostility towards strangers or outsiders, advocacy, col-
leagueship, deference, betrayal, rivalry, leadership, wealth accumulation, schism, and so on.

Large webs of social relations constitute the social entities that
Wiese and Becker called 'plurality patterns' or 'sociative structures'
(p. 79). These are crystallizations or configurations of the more
basic social relations. Although they appear simply as people in
contiguity with one another, they are not merely spatial pluralities
or distributions. Structures of relations cannot be reduced to aggre-
gates of individuals. Relational structures have definite properties
and states that allow us to recognize them as more or less enduring, though they are in constant flux and must not be treated as
substantial entities that exist separately from the sociation of individuals (p. 87). Thus, Mannheim (1934–5), for example, saw
'democratization' as a long-term historical process in which societal
relations of power differentiation between classes are progressively
reduced.

Von Wiese and Becker explored the formation of large collectivities or corporations in terms of a continuum that runs from
crowds and groups to abstract collectivities. This classification is
defined by two dimensions that they called the *duration* and the
abstractness of a social relation. Relational structures are of shorter
or longer duration, and they vary from collections of concrete individuals to abstract entities with a collective consciousness and a distinct identity. A crowd is a relational structure that is both concrete
and short-lived, a group is concrete but longer lasting, while an
abstract collectivity such as a class is both abstract and enduring.

Each type of collectivity can be further analysed along other
dimensions. A classification by size they argued, is the most appropriate to use for crowds and groups. These can, for example, be
seen in terms of the numbers of people involved, leading to a
classification into dyads, triads, medium-sized structures, and larger
structures. As Simmel showed in his own discussion, the size of a
structure gives it particular and distinct characteristics. Dyadic

groups were further classified according to whether they are based on sexuality, friendship, superiority, and so on, while triads were analysed in terms of the significance of the *tertius gaudens*, the third party who gains from divisions among the other participants (see Burt 1992).

Abstract collectivities cannot be so usefully distinguished by the numbers of members that they have. Wiese and Becker held that it was more useful to distinguish between 'primary collectivities' such as families, states, churches (both sects and denominations), estates and classes, and the 'secondary collectivities' that are subsidiary to them. Examples of secondary collectivities are armies, parties, schools, and such diffuse structures as technology, industrial sectors, and the cultural sphere (Wiese–Becker 1932: 443). The larger abstract collectivities include many sets of people who act in common only through the formation of more concrete groups and crowds. The proletariat, for example, is an abstract collectivity whose members may participate in mass action and may form any number of political parties with committees to act in their name.

The work of von Wiese and Becker on the various types of crowd, group, and collectivity has been extended by many other writers. Geiger (1949), for example, was to develop some of these ideas in his formalization of the concept of the 'mass'. It was, however, through the work of the Chicago sociologists that many of these ideas were employed and developed even further. Robert Park, for example, developed a typology of crowds that traced possible directions of movement from 'mobs' through 'gangs' to 'secret societies', providing the basis for such work as that of Thrasher (1927) on the gang as a sociological phenomenon.

The whole complex of relational ideas that were developed in German sociology and in the work of the Chicago school also had a much wider impact in sociology. They were more typically developed in substantive contexts, rather than systematic theories, and led to such important ideas as the ecological model of the city (Park and Burgess 1925), opportunity structure (Cloward and Ohlin 1960), occupational structure (Blau and Duncan 1967), deviance amplification (Young 1971), and electoral competition (Downs 1957), to cite just a few chosen at random.

Relational thinking was particularly strongly developed, however, in the various 'conflict' theories that arose in opposition to the dominance of Parsonian institutional analysis. Dahrendorf (1957) and Rex (1961), for example, looked at the formation of social groups around distributions of power and resources, showing how they enter into competition and conflict with each other over the ways in which these distributions are organized.[8] These arguments owed much to the insights of Marx (see, for example, Marx and Engels 1848) as well as Weber on the structural implications of material resources. Coser's (1956) conflict theory drew rather more on Simmel, looking at how conflict relations among groups can, if multiple and cross-cutting, be bases of solidarity rather than division. Such analyses play down the part played by the cultural, institutional aspects of social structure, emphasizing the need to study such relational phenomena as the division of labour, interdependence, competition, monopolization, oppression, exploitation, and the conflicts and struggles to which these can lead. Lockwood's (1956) influential contribution to this was to show that an analysis of the actual distribution of resources and their relational impact was an essential complement to the normative, institutional analyses of Parsons and his associates.

A recent attempt to explore relational structure in analytical separation from institutional analysis is the work of Peter Blau, who has returned to the classic tradition and has also made important connections with the work of the social network analysts who will be discussed in the following section. Blau (1976, 1977) explicitly aligned himself with Radcliffe-Brown's approach to relational structure and structural form, holding that any concrete social structure can be analysed into a range of different structures according to the 'parameters' that are used to define them. These parameters are the organizing principles that lie behind particular types of social relations, and Blau instances age, sex, and ethnicity as widely applicable relational parameters.

The first step in any structural analysis, Blau held, is to break down a concrete structure into its analytical elements: 'The complex configuration of elements that compose the social structure cannot be understood . . . unless analytical dissection precedes attempts at synthesis' (Blau 1976: 222). In this way, a particular social structure can be analytically divided, and it is likely that these lines of division will also be possible lines of concrete structural *differentiation*. A relational structure, then, is a 'multidimensional space of different social positions among which a population is distributed' (Blau 1977: 4), and the identification of structural parameters allows us to explore this space and the movement of individuals among its different structural locations.

Blau recognized two types of relational parameter and, therefore, two different forms of structural differentiation. 'Nominal'
parameters are those that distinguish locations and subgroups
among which there is no inherent rank order: sex, religion, occupation, and neighbourhood, for example. These nominal parameters involve a 'horizontal' distribution of individuals and are
the bases of what Blau terms the 'heterogeneity' of a population.
'Graduated' parameters, on the other hand, are those that distinguish locations and subgroups in terms of a rank order or continuous variable: age, education, income, and power, for example.
These graduated parameters define a 'vertical' distribution of individuals and are the bases of what Blau terms the 'inequality' of a
population. At the most general level, then, relational structures
can be understood as structures of heterogeneity and inequality,
and a key task in comparative investigation is to identify lines of
heterogeneity and inequality and to examine the connections
between them.

Forms of heterogeneity and inequality are particularly important, Blau argued, whenever they constrain people to associate with
one another in particular ways by limiting the opportunities for
action that are available to them. These associations – patterns of
'sociable intercourse' – 'establish the networks of interpersonal
relations that integrate individuals into cohesive social units',
whether small-scale face-to-face units or larger scale social groupings (1976: 229). In complex societies with numerous lines of social
differentiation, Blau follows Simmel and Coser in anticipating the
existence of multiple cross-cutting ties that link people into their
societies without restricting them to narrow arenas of intense social
attachment (Granovetter 1973; Blau 1976: 234–5). This cross-
cutting of relatively weak ties is central to what Durkheim called
the structure of organic solidarity in modern societies.

Social structures as social networks

Formal, relational sociology borrows heavily from the ideas and
models of geometry, and metaphors of space, distance and mobility
have all been employed. It is important to consider a related strand
of thought that has used actual mathematics to model social processes. Radcliffe-Brown (1937) was one of the earliest to recognize
that the description of social structures would, ultimately, have to
take a mathematical form. The science of society, he held, was in

need of a 'relational mathematics', a non-quantitative calculus of relations, that could grasp the structural features of social life. However, Radcliffe-Brown gave little indication of what kind of mathematics this might be, or of how it might be used. His one example pointed simply to the differential calculus, which looks at the covariation of variables on two or more axes, as in the supply and demand curves of economics. The real pioneers in the use of mathematics to model relational structures were a cluster of small group researchers in the 1940s and 1950s who took up Radcliffe-Brown's challenge and developed an explicitly mathematical approach to the study of networks of social relations.

Cartwright and Harary (Cartwright and Zander 1953; Harary and Norman 1953) were the leading figures in the attempt to use graph theory to construct models of social relations. This work used the terminology of 'points' (agents) and 'lines' (relations) to devise maps of group structure, social cohesion, and social pressure. Echoing some earlier sociometric insights of Moreno (1934), they advocated the construction of sociograms to represent social relations and urged the employment of formal mathematical procedures to analyse these sociograms. George Homans (1950) began to build on these insights and to integrate them with the results of anthropological work in an attempt to produce a counter-sociology to the then dominant framework of Parsonian normative functionalism.[9] His work centred on the claim that social relations varied in terms of their frequency, duration, and direction, and that the task of sociological analysis was to chart and then to explain networks of social interaction built in terms of these parameters. At about the same time, a group of British social anthropologists began to build a more systematic and formal framework of analysis from Radcliffe-Brown's idea of social structure as 'the network of actually existing relations'. Barnes (1954) and Bott (1955, 1956) modelled kinship and community structures as social networks, pointing to the need to study the degree of 'connectedness' found in networks of points and lines.

These strands were forged together in the work of White (1963) in the United States and Mitchell (1969) in Britain. Mitchell saw social network analysis as a distinct sociological approach that took the structure of social relations as its specific object of concern. Drawing on the mathematical ideas of graph theory, he saw concrete 'multiplex' social relations as requiring decomposition into their constituent forms of social relation. They could then be analysed in terms of their reciprocity, intensity, and durability, and in terms of the overall 'density' or cohesion of the social network. White, meanwhile, had begun to use algebraic methods to express structures of relations, and he brought together a group of mathematically orientated structural analysts who made the crucial advances that led to the emergence of formal social network analysis as a distinct research paradigm (Mullins 1973; Wellman 1988). Under White's influence, Granovetter (1974) and others employed increasingly sophisticated mathematics to explore structures of social relations.[10]

The basic presumption of social network analysis is that sociograms of points and lines can be used to represent agents and their social relations. The pattern of connections among the lines in a sociogram represents the relational structure of a society or social group, and the mathematical analysis of the sociogram yields information about this structure of social relations. Two points that are connected by a line are said to be 'adjacent' to one another, and the total set of points to which any particular point is adjacent is called its 'neighbourhood'. The number of other points that lie within the neighbourhood of a point comprise its 'degree' – its degree of connection – and this is one of the most important measures in social network analysis. In small group research, for example, the degree of an individual has often been taken as an indicator of his or her popularity or power. Points may, of course, be connected indirectly by a sequence of lines, rather than being directly connected by a single line. The 'length' of this sequence of lines – the number of distinct links that it contains – is, then, a measure of the 'distance' between two points. A friend of a friend of a friend, for example, is a more distant contact than a direct personal friend.

From these basic concepts – modified to take account of the strength and direction of a social relation – social network analysts have built more complex structural concepts. The 'density' of a network, for example, is the proportion of all possible relations that have actually been established by the actors. Four individuals can – in principle – be connected by a total of six social relations, and a network in which four of these relations exist is denser than one in which only one or two are found. Density is a particularly important measure of the overall cohesion or solidarity of a social group, but social network analysts have also developed concepts for exploring the fragmentation of a network. A network may, for example, comprise a number of distinct 'components' or overlapping 'cliques'. A component is a section of a network that is internally connected but that has no external connections. Components are mutually exclusive, and individuals can be members of only one, or of no components of their network. Cliques, on the other hand, are parts of a network that have a high level of internal connection but that may also be connected, less strongly, to other parts of the network. Thus, cliques may overlap in their membership, and clique analysis is a principal way in which overlapping group memberships and cross-cutting solidarities – a central concern for Simmel – can be explored.

Nadel's early work (1957) pointed the way to some extensions of these ideas by using algebraic methods to disclose the 'ordered arrangement' of social relations into structural 'roles' and positions.[11] Social structures are 'networks' of such relations and can be studied in terms of their 'coherence' or 'interlocking' into systems (Nadel 1957: 12, 20).[12] These ideas have been taken up by a number of White's students who have examined the 'substitutability' or 'structural equivalence' of those who are embedded in similar sets of social relations (Lorrain and White 1971). Those who are connected in the same kinds of ways to the same kinds of others – even though these may be different others – are, in a structural sense, interchangeable with one another. Two men with similar relations to children, for example, may be structurally equivalent as 'fathers': they will face similar constraints, have similar experiences, and will be likely to respond in similar ways. This is most clearly the case when the position of 'father' is culturally recognized and institutionalized as a social role, the normative expectations of others reinforcing the relational constraints that people experience. Work in social network analysis, however, has explicitly attempted to distinguish the institutional and relational aspects of this process, holding that structurally equivalent sets of social relations may be identifiable even when they do not correspond to institutionalized social roles. The structural analysis of a sociogram, then, can involve the identification of the system of structurally equivalent positions that constitute its social structure. This is, in Radcliffe-Brown's words, the discovery of its structural form (Boorman and White 1976; White *et al.* 1976; Burt 1982).

Social network analysis, then, has systematically developed the relational focus of the German social theorists and the British social anthropologists, seeing structures of social relations as defining a multidimensional social space within which agents can be located and their actions explained (Laumann 1966; Freeman 1983). It has been possible here to sketch only the basic features of this approach, ignoring its subtleties and refinements (Berkowitz 1982; Scott 2000). It has, however, increasingly been recognized as offering a comprehensive framework for the analysis of relational structure that complements the institutional approach to social structure and other approaches to sociological understanding (Emirbayer and Goodwin 1994; Emirbayer 1997; Somers 1998). Social network analysis is not, in itself, a specific theory or set of theories. It is a general orientation to the analysis of social structure combined with a series of mathematical concepts and the technical methods required to use them in sociological analysis. Like formal sociology and structural functionalism, it sensitizes researchers to particular features of social structure and it informs the construction of specific theories. We will conclude this chapter with an illustration of the ways in which such relational ideas have been used to highlight the non-institutional aspects of social structure.

The case of urban conflicts and class conflicts

We have traced ideas of relational structure, showing how its analysis differs from that of institutional structure. These ideas can be illustrated by considering some important analyses of urban processes and class conflicts in terms of their spatial arrangement and the distribution of resources. We will look at the use of relational structure in the work of the Chicago school of urban sociology and its extension to other urban and regional situations.

Park's most important role was in placing the relational ideas of Simmel in the context of a larger relational view of urban processes in contemporary societies, building a powerful and sophisticated set of concepts for the analysis of urban conflict and change. Writing with Burgess, Park argued that the city had to be understood as more than simply a physical space. It is a cultural, institutional reality – 'a state of mind, a body of customs and traditions' (Park and Burgess 1925: 2) – but it is also a relational reality produced by those who live in it. A city is, for example, an ecological and economic unit that is shaped by its size and by the resources contained within it (its morphology) and by the actions of association and dissociation of the individuals and groups that use these resources to organize their lives within that space.

The relational structure of the city as a social system comprises a pattern of neighbourhoods and segregated areas that are built through competitive struggles and that each have their own distinctive social characteristics. There will be, for example, prosperous and poor districts, business districts, neighbourhoods in which particular ethnic minorities or occupations are concentrated, and so on. This kind of structure was depicted in the famous concentric zone model for large cities such as Chicago (Park and Burgess 1925: 51). In this model, an inner business district is surrounded by a zone of transition, a zone of working family homes, a zone of affluent residents, and, on its fringes, a suburban commuter zone. The struggles of groups for resources and opportunities as the city expands produces, and then reproduces, this social structure. Such a social system is, Park and Burgess argued, 'a kind of psychophysical mechanism' that is 'analogous to the anabolic and katabolic processes of metabolism in the body' (p. 53). This reiteration of the metaphor of the social body was to emphasize the non-normative character of the processes identified. While not going as far as Schäffle in his view of the social body, Park and Burgess sought to emphasize the distinctive circuits, flows, and interdependencies in social relations that defined the shape of a city and that underpinned the subcultures and specialized social institutions that grew up in its various zones.

This relational view of urban processes has provided a sophisticated key for understanding the relational structure of contemporary societies. Whatever doubts there may be about the evidential base for the specific model in relation to particular cities, the formal, relational methodology that it embodies has had a wide application. In addition to leading studies of Chicago itself (Zorbaugh 1929; Cavan 1928; Drake and Cayton 1945), it was used in a study of Birmingham by Rex and Moore (1969).

John Rex (1961) used similar ideas in a larger 'conflict' model of society. He argued that it was necessary to complement institutional analysis with an investigation of the ways in which inter-class relations are built into a variety of systems of domination through the actions of the conflict groups that struggle with each other at the societal level. In a 'ruling class situation', for example, one class dominates the whole society, determines the shape of its social institutions, and perpetuates its power over one or more subordinate classes. In the 'truce situation', on the other hand, there is a balance of power between two more or less equally matched social classes, and a whole series of negotiated compromises are established. Finally, the 'revolutionary situation' is one where subordinate classes have mobilized to resist the power of a dominant class and initiate a transformation in the social order.

The power of this kind of conflict model for exploring social relations is apparent from the interesting application of it by Hechter (1975) to regional and intranational conflicts. Hechter used a model of core–periphery relations drawn from the work of Frank (1969), to understand British national development. The core of a society, he argued, comprises the territory of its political centre and is the basis of its dominant cultural and economic groups. The power of the core extends to the subordinate areas that comprise the peripheral territories. Economic transactions between core and periphery, Hechter argued, establish the economic dependence of the periphery on the core, through unequal exchange and exploitation, and are the basis of continued economic backwardness and political subordination. In Britain, he traced the formation of 'English' core territories and subordinate 'Celtic' peripheries, seeing a conflict between them as rooted in their relations of dependence, inequality, and exploitation.

The case of world systems

World system analysis has developed, largely though not exclusively, from the work of Wallerstein (1974), as an explicitly relational approach to the global structure of social relations in the modern period. Wallerstein held that the modern world system of intersocietal relations was not defined by overarching political or cultural institutions, as had been the case with earlier 'world empires', but through the complex interdependencies of an economic division of labour. Political, cultural, and other social institutions played their part in the organization of the world system, but its most important characteristics were the non-institutional relations of exploitation and hegemony that result from the network of economic transactions that bind individuals, business enterprises, and nation states together.

Wallerstein's model identifies three zones within the modern world system: the core, the periphery, and the semi-periphery. The core areas are those parts of Europe, North America, and East Asia where capitalism and then industrialism transformed pre-capitalist economies and allowed these societies to expand through their dominance in international trade and production. Those areas of Central and South America, Africa, and Asia into which these economies expanded became the peripheral zones of the world system, providing commodities and resources to the core economies in forced and unequal exchange relations. Semi-peripheral zones are intermediate between core and periphery, exploiting those in the periphery but being exploited by those in the core (Emmanuel 1972; Chase-Dunn 1989). World system analysts have traced the changing balance of power within the core as the hegemonic position passed from Britain to the United States, and they have looked at the implications of this for the degree of exploitation that exists between core and periphery. The rapid economic development of the Tiger economies of East Asia from periphery to semi-periphery, for example, has been seen as reflecting their sponsorship by the United States after the Second World War and the subsequent rise of Japan to a core position and the construction of a strong 'Pacific Rim' economy (So and Chiu 1995; Applebaum and Henderson 1992).

Investigations of trading networks have disclosed such things as the changing patterns of centrality of particular national economies and global regions and the formation of distinct trading blocs and spheres of influence. Nation states are increasingly drawn into the major trading blocs, each of which has its own internal structure of relations between core and peripheral participants (Su 1999). Within each economy there are characteristic structures of corporate control and trading that evolve in response to the changing global structure (Scott 1997).

It has also been shown how political relations of dominance and hegemony are associated with these economic relations in a complex global political economy. Moves towards political union, as in parts of Europe, and patterns of military conflict reflect changing patterns of global hegemony in economic and political relations and the competition among nation states. Drawing on such work, some analysts have sought to predict the likelihood of warfare between core states in the twenty-first century (Chase-Dunn and Podobnik 1999).

One growing area of research, however, has concerned the extent to which these global relations are able to be institutionalized in new cultural and political institutions. Meyer and others, for example, show how insights from new institutionalism can complement an analysis of relational structure in the world system (see Meyer *et al*. 1997).

In summary, through both of our substantive examples we have tried to show that it is possible to identify a facet of social organization, relational structure, that is distinct from institutional structure. This is irreducible to institutional structure but, like institutional structure, it has no substantial existence separate from the actions of the individuals and groups that reproduce it. In the words of Godelier:

> Social relations are not things. They do not exist without human intervention and action producing and reproducing them each day – which does not mean that they are always reproduced in a form identical to that of yesterday or the day before yesterday. All relations are realities in flux and motion, and in this movement they are daily deformed, altered or eroded to a greater or lesser degree, vanishing or metamorphosing.
>
> (Godelier 1984: 18)

While distinct from institutional structures, relational structures are not unconnected with them. The question of how best these two facets of social structure can be put together has introduced a vast realm of conceptual difficulties. The lack of appreciation of these difficulties is in part responsible for the focus on either one or the other in many discussions on social structure. In the next chapter we will examine this issue as we try to come to grips with the problems of representing and linking together distinct different *levels* of structure.

Levels of Structure

In the last two chapters we discussed the principal ways in which social structure has been understood: relational structure and institutional structure. We have argued that these ideas are complementary, though this is not to say that they can easily be combined into a single theory. In fact, attempts to do this have led to many misunderstandings. Sometimes, one aspect of social structure has been seen as causally determining the other, making one fundamental and the other merely epiphenomenal. Other attempts to bring the two ideas together have seen them as expressions of some common structuring principle, making them completely isomorphic (Archer 1988).

This problem of how to connect relational structure with institutional structure is, in fact, one aspect of a much larger issue in structural analysis. This is the question of what can be called ontological depth: the layering, nesting, or embedding of aspects of social structure one in relation to another. How are the surface features of social structure – those that are most easily and directly observable – related to the wider and deeper features of social structure that are less easily observable? The roles of husband and wife and their interactions with each other, to take a simple example, are embedded in the larger structure of the family. Family structures may, in turn, be elements in an extended kinship system that is, in its turn, part of a tribal structure of communal relations and institutions.

The terminology that we have used to make this point highlights the difficulties that sociologists have had in conceptualizing the ontological depth of social organization. We have used such terms as 'surface' and 'deeper', 'embedded' and 'nested', 'larger' and 'wider', and so on. These words point to different ways of grasping the *levels* of social structure that give ontological depth to social life. The most influential way of formulating the question of onto-logical depth has been the distinction between 'surface structure' and 'deep structure', and this terminology has been used by adherents to a large variety of theoretical positions.

This way of posing the problem originated in Lévi-Strauss's (1968) critique of Radcliffe-Brown's view of social structure as actual patterns of social relations among people and the 'structural forms' that these take. Lévi-Strauss adopted a geological metaphor, arguing that this kind of analysis limited its attention to the surface of social life and failed to investigate the more important things that were happening under the surface. Sociological analysis, Lévi-Strauss held, must relate the surface structure of social life to its underlying, deep structure. This argument has, in recent years, been explored in critical realist philosophy of science, where Roy Bhaskar (1975, 1979, 1989) has argued the need for a more complex understanding of the relations among different levels of reality and to see it as 'stratified'.[1]

In this chapter, we will explore the metaphors that have been used to explore the relationship between surface structures and deep structures. The one that comes closest to implementing Lévi-Strauss's geological imagery is that which divides social structure into 'base' and 'superstructure' levels. This metaphor was most clearly developed in the Marxist tradition and, of course, predates Lévi-Strauss's own work – it was, in fact, one of his main sources of inspiration. We will look at the insights achieved and the problems faced by those who have used this metaphor. The second metaphor that we will discuss is that which divides social structure into 'system' and 'subsystem' levels. This metaphor breaks with the physical, geological imagery of the base/superstructure idea and is able to highlight certain features of social structure that it fails to see. However, it, too, has conceptual problems that limit its usefulness. We will look finally at how structural analysis has begun to go beyond these two metaphors, using the new metaphor of the differentiated fields of a social space.

Base and superstructure

The base/superstructure model is one in which two principal levels of social structure are identified and a causal relationship is seen as holding between them. One level (the base) determines or conditions the other (the superstructure). At its crudest, this may involve a simple determinism in which the features of the superstructure are seen as mere effects of the base. In most variants, however, some autonomy is recognized for the superstructure and there is an attempt to theorize the limits to this autonomy. Most formulations of this model have seen the relational structure of a society as forming its base and have ascribed primary causal significance to this. A leading example is provided by the work of Durkheim, who saw collective representations as determined by collective relationships.

In his work, Durkheim used a two-level model of social structure in which collective relationships were a 'substratum', while collective representations formed a 'superstructure' erected on top of it. Durkheim's discussion of this model highlights the difficulties and ambiguities that have been apparent in all subsequent discussions. At times, it seems that Durkheim was suggesting that there is a temporal relationship of causality between the two aspects of social structure. In *The Division of Labour in Society*, for example, he argued that changes in the relational structure of interdependencies, defining the shift from mechanical to organic solidarity, precede a corresponding shift from a repressive to a restitutive collective conscience (Durkheim 1893). However, this was not consistently seen as a simple one-way causal relationship between substratum and superstructure. Durkheim held, for example, that collective representations formed a partially autonomous realm that was, to a degree, able to follow its own principles. Collective representations

> have the power to attract and repel each other and to form amongst themselves various syntheses, which are determined by their natural affinities, and not by the condition of their matrix [of collective relationships]. As a consequence, the new representations born of these syntheses have the same nature; they are immediately caused by other collective representations and not by this or that characteristic of the social structure.
>
> (Durkheim 1898: 31)

Unfortunately, Durkheim never managed to demonstrate convincingly how this causation and relative autonomy was to be understood. Nor did he formulate the principles that might govern the autonomous dynamics of collective representations.

It was in Marx's work that the metaphor of base and superstructure received its classic statement. Although he explored neither social relations nor social institutions and representations with the same rigour as had Durkheim, he did produce a powerful conceptualization of the relationship between them that he used in a number of his own studies.

From Hegelian philosophy, Marx took over the idea that social structure was to be seen as an organized whole, a 'totality' that develops over time (Jay 1984: 62–3). Hegel's understanding of the social totality as a social mind – a national or communal folk spirit – was not unimportant for Marx, who saw such forms of social consciousness as forming the ideology or ruling ideas of an epoch. However, Marx's treatment of these ideas and representations depended upon his view that the historical totality had to be understood also, and more fundamentally, as a material totality. The two aspects are combined together in the structural whole or totality that is social life.

Social life has its roots in the material process through which human labour is organized, and this is a structure of social relations. Marx added the complication that these social relations are to be conceptualized as specifically economic relations that are, in turn, to be seen as relations of production. Although Marx developed his analysis in terms of these economic relations of production, this particular aspect of his argument is not essential to the questions that we are considering here. What is crucial is his *method*, which sees a social structure as divided into a 'material' base of social relations and a superstructure of social representations and institutions, and his suggestion that social relations can be hierarchically differentiated (see Figure 5. 1). Marx's distinct contribution to the analysis of social structure was to use the base/superstructure metaphor to weld together elements of the idealism of Hegel and the materialism of the British political economists into a coherent theoretical framework. This metaphor allowed Marx not only to distinguish between different aspects of social structure, but also to see them as distinct 'levels' whose interconnections could be established.

The clearest formulation of his base/superstructure model is to be found in the 1859 Preface to *A Contribution to the Critique of Political Economy*. There he wrote that:

In the social production of their life, men enter into definite relations that are indispensable and independent of their will, relations of

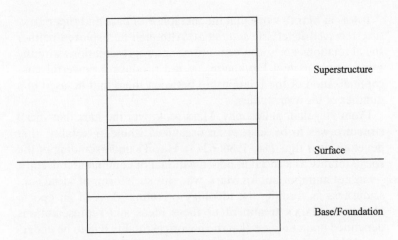

Figure 5.1 Ontological depth: base and superstructure

> production which correspond to a definite state of development of
> their material forces. The sum total of these relations of production
> constitutes the economic structure of society, the real foundations on
> which rises the legal and political superstructure and to which corre-
> spond definite forms of social consciousness.
>
> (Marx 1859: 159–60)

Material production, he argued, always occurs in specific types of
social relations, which he called relations of production. The
relations of production in a society comprise its *economic structure.*
The economic structure combines these social relations, which
shape the productive activities of individuals, with the material
resources that make that productive activity possible. These
material resources Marx called the 'forces of production'. They are
the land, machinery, factories, raw materials, labour power, and
technical knowledge whose social distribution comprises what
Durkheim was later to call a social morphology.[2] The economic
structure, then, combines relations and resources.

The social relations of production are essentially relations of
ownership and control of the means of production, and they establish class relations between categories of individuals who stand in
differing relations to the means of production. The existence of a
class of capitalists, as owners or controllers of the means of material
production, for example, implies the simultaneous existence of a

class of labourers who have no such possession and are forced to work for the property owners in order to meet their own subsistence needs.

The economic structure, Marx went on to say, formed the base or 'real foundation' of social organization. There was also, however, the other, more idealistic, aspect of social structure that he divided into the 'legal and political superstructure' and the forms of social consciousness to which these 'correspond'. The social institutions of the legal and political superstructure, and the cultural forms of consciousness that inform them, are intricately connected to one another, but these social institutions were not seen by Marx in exclusively cultural terms. The legal and constitutional norms that define the state apparatus, for example, must also be seen as involving relations of coercion and repression. At its most general, then, the legal and political superstructure comprises all those elements of control and repression through which a dominant class of owners maintains and preserves its powers and interests. The laws of private property, for example, are seen as the legal codification or 'expression' of the relations of production that constitute patterns of ownership and control, and government is seen as the means through which the interests of a dominant class are given voice.

This point was clarified in Althusser's discussion of the state apparatus, which introduced a distinction between the 'repressive' and the 'ideological' aspects of the state (Althusser 1971: 1–60). The repressive aspect of the state consists of relations of direct and naked coercion that are organized through the police, the military, the prisons, and so on. The ideological aspect, on the other hand, is based on the internalization of those worldviews, understandings, and conceptual systems that legitimate these social relations. This socialization occurs through such social institutions as schooling, religion, trade unionism, political association, the mass media, and the law.

The other component of the superstructure that Marx referred to was the 'forms of social consciousness', or the 'idealistic' superstructure. By this he meant a 'superstructure of distinct and peculiarly formed sentiments, illusions, modes of thought and views of life' (Marx 1852: 117; see also Marx and Engels 1846: 64). There is a widespread tendency to see this superstructure of ideas as an 'ideological' superstructure, though Larrain (1979: 50) has pointed out that Marx never used the expression 'ideological superstructure'.

When Marx used the word 'ideology' he referred always to particular 'distortions' and 'inversions', and these need not apply to an entire idealistic superstructure (Mannheim 1929). What is more, he went on to argue that not all cognitive errors should be understood as ideological in origin. An error can, for example, be a simple factual or logical mistake.

The base/superstructure model has often been read as a form of economic determinism. In such a model, the legal and political structure would merely crystallize the interests of the economically dominant class, while the so-called 'ideological superstructure' would 'reflect', 'echo' or produce 'illusions', 'inverted images' and 'fantasies'. This leads to the belief that the particular configurations of the legal and political superstructure, along with forms of consciousness, can be deduced from the material forms of economic organization: social institutions and representations are simply derived from the social (economic) relations. Raymond Williams (1977: 95–100) has highlighted the difficulties that the base/superstructure model has in handling cultural phenomena when it tends to see the superstructure as a 'reflection' of the underlying base. This leads the cultural aspects of economic production to be all but ignored, and the material or relational aspects of politics and ideology to be minimized.

Although Marx explicitly states that forms of consciousness and the institutions that they inform are historically specific and socially constituted, he is not so clear about how this social conditioning works. While it is true that Marx equated social relations with economic relations, he did not reduce the superstructure to a causal effect of the economic base. He was, in fact, very concerned to theorize the autonomy of the superstructure, though his comments are suggestive rather than definitive. He stressed, for example, how closely interwoven are the social relations and their representations. They were seen as intricately interwoven into the material practices of individuals and as arising directly from the lived experiences of the members of the various classes.

This point was developed in Marx's analysis of what he called 'commodity fetishism'. This describes the belief that commodities exist as independent 'things' with powers of their own. It occurs when individuals fail to realize that the relations between these things – for example, price relations among goods in the market – are merely the superficial forms of appearance of the actual social relations of production in which they are involved.[3] This fetishism does not involve a simple error of perception or a failure of understanding. It is an inevitable consequence of the material relations within which people live. This ideological way of seeing commodities is an integral feature of the relations of production of a capitalist society. It is a necessary, systemic feature of the social organization of production.

This points to the difficulty that Marx had in sustaining the idea of separate spheres (base and superstructure) between which there were causal relations. If consciousness is an integral part of the lived experience of social relations, it cannot be separated off as a discrete, and secondary, chunk of reality. Nevertheless, Marx often tends to imply exactly this kind of separation. In *The German Ideology*, for example, Marx and Engels wrote that

> The ideas of the ruling class are in every epoch the ruling ideas: i.e., the class which is the ruling material force of society, is at the same time its ruling intellectual force. The class which has the material means of material production at its disposal, has control at the same time over the means of mental production ... generally speaking, the ideas of those who lack the means of mental production are subject to it.
>
> (Marx and Engels 1846: 64)

This implies that the entire 'idealistic superstructure' is a mere reflection of the interests of the ruling class, and is brought into alignment with these interests through their deliberate and intentional actions. Ideas and forms of consciousness, along with the social institutions that they inform, involve what orthodox Marxism called 'false consciousness'. Ideology is false in so far as it is imposed on people from without, through a process of socialization and indoctrination that undermines the validity of their own views and favours those of the holders of power. Institutional structure, then, would reflect a dominant ideology, an argument that parallels that of those normative functionalists and conflict theorists who saw the possibility that social norms could be imposed by a minority over a majority (Abercrombie *et al.* 1979). This view also implies that there are no independent rational principles governing institutional change. In his 'Preface' (1859), for example, Marx contrasted changes in the economic base, 'which can be determined with the precision of natural science', with those in 'the legal, political, religious, aesthetic or philosophic' spheres that showed no such logic. These are seen as irrational and arbitrary changes that can be understood only as 'reflections' of an economic logic.

Both Marx and Engels were profoundly dissatisfied with this deterministic model, no matter how often they kept coming back to its relatively simple formulations. They constantly sought to recognize the 'autonomy' of the superstructure and its freedom from complete determination by its economic base. In the 'Preface', for example, Marx immediately qualified his strongly determinist statement by saying that the mode of production 'conditions the social, political and intellectual life process in general' and not in all its particulars (Marx 1859: 160). Engels argued vigorously against the mechanical determination thesis, with which he and Marx had come to be identified. He argued quite convincingly that neither he nor Marx saw the functioning of the economic structure as a simple mono-causal process of determination. In his famous letter to Bloch, Engels wrote that

> . . . the determining element in history is *ultimately* the production and reproduction in real life. More than this neither Marx nor I have ever asserted. If therefore somebody twists this into the statement that the economic element is the *only* determining one, he transforms it into a meaningless, abstract and absurd phrase.
>
> (Engels 1890: 475)

Engels suggested that there is a reciprocal interaction between elements in the base and elements in the superstructure. He likened the complexity of this interaction to that of 'innumerable intersecting forces, an infinite series of parallelograms of forces which give rise to one resultant – the historical event' (Engels 1890: 476). Social structure itself is the 'resultant' of these forces. He maintained, however, that, within this complex interplay of causal forces, the 'economic movement' remains the strongest and the most decisive, even if elements from the superstructure might, in some cases, be predominant in shaping specific historical events. The causal influence of economic relations prevails 'in the last instance', though not necessarily in every specific event. What remains unclear in these remarks is the nature of the mechanisms that can align the economic structure with the superstructure 'in the last instance'. If the superstructure is not just a mere 'reflex' or 'expression' of the economic structure, then what social mechanisms or processes allow them to be simultaneously both aligned and relatively independent?[4]

Marx has provided the clearest and most influential formulation of the base/superstructure model that was glimpsed in Durkheim and that has been applied in a wide range of studies. Writers differ on the question of whether the base is to be understood in purely economic terms, in political terms, as a composite political economy, or in terms of wider social relations, and they also differ on whether this base is to be seen in exclusively relational terms or as combining relational and institutional elements. Nevertheless, the influence of a broad conception of a causally linked base and superstructure, with the base firmly grounded in social morphology, is clear.

There are, however, major difficulties with the model. The twists and turns in the attempts of Marx and Engels to clarify the nature of the causal relations involved have not yielded a satisfactory and coherent account of the relationship between the various levels of social structure. The roots of these problems lie in the analogy with physical structure that is at the heart of the model. The concept of structure, as we showed in Chapter 2, originated in physical and architectural ideas, and it was gradually generalized to other contexts where physical correlates of 'buildings' were not always apparent. Use of the physical analogy implies that the base exists somehow separately from, and 'below', the superstructure that it supports. The base provides the sub-surface 'foundations' on which the visible superstructure is constructed. The superstructure stands on the surface and rises above it, being supported, and prevented from collapse, by its base. Spelling out these implications highlights the limitations of the metaphor of base and superstructure for the social sciences. There is no 'outside' or 'below' in the social world. The ontological depth of the social world is not a physical depth, but a virtual depth that can be uncovered by a progressive refinement in intellectual focus but that cannot, ultimately, be grasped in physical language.

Systems and subsystems

Marx's conception of the connection between deep structure and surface structure, in terms of a base/superstructure model, gave primacy to social relations, and within them to economic relations. The other influential view of the connection has given primacy to social institutions and has seen these in terms of a system/subsystem model. This view is most particularly associated with Parsons, and it has inspired a whole school of 'functionalist' systems theories. Most recently, these same ideas have been developed in the form of the 'neofunctionalism' of Alexander and Luhmann. These writers moved from their initial structural functional approaches to broader systems theories. They took their inspiration from the development of general systems theories in a number of sciences from the 1950s, though systems ideas go back as far as the biological analogies used by Spencer and Schäffle.

Beginning with ideas in information science and the building of computer systems, general systems theory suggested new ways of understanding organization and structure in biological and then human systems (von Bertalanffy 1973). Central to these theories was the idea that living entities had a form of organization that could be understood in terms of processes of control that maintained a distinction between the system and its environment and that allowed the system to be differentiated into autonomous subsystems. The analytical movement from environment to system and to subsystem involved a shift to levels of greater ontological depth and seemed, to many people, to offer more scope than the base/superstructure model. Greater analytical sophistication seemed to be offered by two key features of general systems theories. First, the physical imagery of 'above' and 'below' was abandoned in favour of a more conceptual imagery of the nesting and embedding of systems within one another. Second, this imagery pointed to the possibility of exploring greater ontological depths through the identification of sub-subsystems, sub-sub-subsystems, and so on, each with its own distinct level of organized complexity.

Parsons saw the driving forces in the articulation of systems and subsystems as the strains and tensions that they experienced as they adapted to those other systems that make up their environments. Adaptation was not seen as a teleological goal to which systems are somehow orientated, but as an unintended consequence of behavioural responses. Parsons held that coexisting systems must accommodate themselves to their mutual effects on each other. The adaptations that they make determine the structure of the overarching, encompassing system, and this structure will involve varying degrees of compatibility and autonomy among its constituent elements.

Parsons began from an initial differentiation of systems and subsystems in relation to what he called the action system, and he showed how the intellectual division of labour between the various human sciences can be understood in terms of their concerns for different subsystems of action. An action system, Parsons argued, is any system through which cultural representations and symbols are formed into meaningful intentions and are given expression in concrete situations. A major concern for biology is to explore this from the standpoint of organisms – organic systems – looking at genetic structure and its influence on the anatomical and physiological mechanisms that underpin all meaningful action by organisms. Psychology, on the other hand, looks at the learning process through which such organisms are able to form the mental structures that constitute 'personality systems'. Organic systems and personality systems, therefore, are contained within the action system as two of its subsystems. Parsons recognized a specific object for the social sciences as the 'social system', and he saw this as yet a further subsystem of action. A social system comprises structures of specifically *social* action, understood as processes of interaction in which the involvement of two or more individuals creates a 'problem of order' or integration separate from the integration of each individual's personality. The final subsystem of action that Parsons identified is culture, the system of shared symbols and ideas that underpin mental and social structures.

A system of action, then, consists of organic, personality, social, and cultural subsystems. Parsons saw each of these subsystems as concerned with particular 'functional' aspects of the encompassing action system. The specifically functionalist aspect of Parsons's work need not concern us here, as we are concerned with the method that he used to distinguish types of structure. This method involves a recognition that subsystems are embedded or nested within surrounding systems, and Parsons represented this in his famous diagram of 'boxes' (see Figure 5. 2). Each square box represents a system, and boxes that are wholly contained within a larger box are subsystems of it. Parsons's argument could just as easily have been represented as concentric circles. What is important is that he used a non-physical metaphor to understand ontological depth. Deep structures do not exist 'below' surface structures; they are laterally embedded within them. A subsystem of action, therefore, is 'an analytical aspect abstractable from the total action processes' (Parsons 1966: 8, emphasis removed) but not existing in any concrete sense separately from it.

For Parsons, a social system is a subsystem of action in which structured interactions are formed. These social structures, as we showed in Chapter 3, are cultural in character, as they involve the

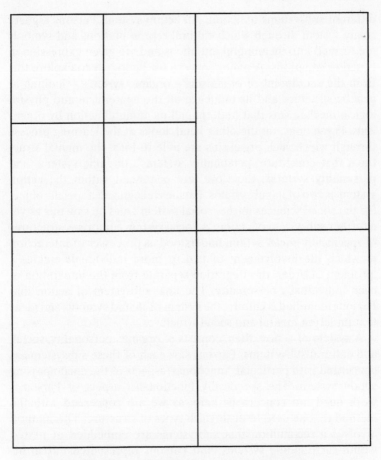

Figure 5.2 Ontological depth: system and subsystem

symbolic organization of action. Parsons went on to look at the
ways in which distinct subsystems can be seen as embedded within
social systems, each of these involving a specific type of social structure. The core subsystem of any social system is what Parsons called
– in the case of a whole society – its 'societal community'. This is a
normative ordering of social positions and their associated roles,
organized through legal and customary norms. It is a systematic
combination of these norms into an institutional framework that
comprises a 'complex network of interpenetrating collectivities and
collective loyalties' (Parsons 1971b: 13). It is expressed particularly
in forms of social stratification, but also in specialized institutions

that sustain and support other social subsystems. These other sub-systems include, most importantly, the 'polity' which comprises social structures that are concerned with the organization of co-ordinated action for the attainment of collectively significant goals; and the 'economy' which comprises social institutions that regulate technological processes and the processes of production, distri-bution, and consumption.

Having got to this point, he then showed how it is possible to dig deeper into the levels of social structure to identify further subsys-tems. The societal community, for example, he saw as divisible into subsystems of collective representations, norms, collectivities, and roles. Similarly, he looked at subsystems of economies and polities, such as their organizational, investment, administrative, and legis-lative systems. Each of these, he argued, could be analysed systemically as subsystems, and they too can, in their turn, be deconstructed into their own subsystems.

Many of these particular claims are specific to Parsons's formu-lation of systems theory, and his arguments show clearly his empha-sis on institutional structure and the marginalization of relational structure. The general methodology of structural analysis that he sets out, however, has been adapted by other writers who have tried to investigate levels of structure in a way that avoids the over-simplifications of the base/superstructure model.

Luhmann, for example, has developed this in an ingenious way. He saw the crucial step in the development of systems theory as being the replacement of an earlier terminology of 'parts' and 'wholes' by that of 'systems' and 'environments', which allowed a much clearer formulation of the idea of system differentiation. A differentiated system is not simply composed of parts – the parts are themselves systems (subsystems) and they collectively form the internal environment of the whole system (Luhmann 1975: 7, 18. See also Buckley 1967).

Systems, Luhmann emphasizes, are things that establish bound-aries and, therefore, differentiate themselves from their environ-ments. System differentiation is this same process of boundary maintenance occurring within systems. This results in a 'hierar-chization' of systems: 'subsystems can differentiate into further subsystems and . . . a transitive relation of containment within con-tainment emerges' (Luhmann 1975: 19). That is, systems are nested, embedded or contained within environing systems, producing a hierarchy of levels of social structure.

Habermas: a partial synthesis?

We have, so far, looked separately at the two principal views on
levels of social structure, and it is worth pausing to look at the work
of someone who has attempted to combine them into a single
model. The work of Habermas is a sophisticated attempt to do this,
and his influential work has suggested a possible direction forward
for structural analysis in sociology.

Habermas attempts to recast the Marxist model of base
and superstructure by incorporating arguments from Parsons,
Luhmann, and other systems theorists.[5] His most sustained effort
at this synthesis is his two-volume work, *The Theory of Communicative Action* (Habermas 1981a and b). At the heart of his theory is
a distinction between the aspect of social structure which is generated by communicative action and that which is generated by
purposive action. Communicative action, he holds, is primarily
orientated towards the attainment of mutual understanding
between the participants in a system of action. Actors relate to each
other in terms of their shared normative expectations and, for their
actions to proceed, they must agree upon a common definition of
the situation. Purposive action, on the other hand, is orientated
towards the attainment of goals in the most rational and effective
way. Actors relate to each other in strategic and calculative ways.
Concrete actions, of course, combine both of these orientations to
varying degrees. Nevertheless, Habermas holds that they may be
usefully distinguished as ideal types. He sees each type of action as
generating distinct forms of social structure, and he holds that it is
useful to distinguish these, despite the fact that any concrete social
structure will combine them together. Indeed, a central tenet of
Habermas's argument is that actual societies show varying degrees
of *differentiation* between the aspects of social structure.

Habermas sees the aspect of social structure that is generated by
communicative actions as an 'institutional framework', and he
argues that this forms a sociocultural 'lifeworld' that organizes day-
to-day experiences. It comprises 'the legitimate orders through
which participants regulate their memberships in social groups and
thereby secure solidarity' (Habermas 1981b: 138). He sees Parsons
and the neofunctionalists as having made major contributions to
the analysis of this aspect of social structure, and he would see the
ideas that we have discussed in Chapter 3 as being fundamental to
an account of institutional structure. He aims to show, however,

that a full understanding of norms and symbolic communication requires, in addition, ideas taken from phenomenological and symbolic interactionist theories.

Purposive actions generate structures of instrumental social relations that, in so far as they can be understood in non-normative terms, can be seen as purely relational structures. Habermas takes far less account of the particular approaches to relational structure that we discussed in Chapter 4, except for those that have been directly taken up in the Marxist tradition (see also Horkheimer *et al.* 1956). He specifically follows the Marxian view of the base in stressing the primacy of economic and, increasingly, of political relations. This relational base is a political economy that Habermas calls, rather loosely and misleadingly, the 'system'. Purposive social actions, he holds, are not aligned through social norms but through the use of money and power, and the base system is coordinated through the flow of these 'steering media'.

The extent to which the relational structure of the base system is actually separated from the institutional superstructure of the life-world is, Habermas argues, quite variable from one society to another, and the relationship between them can change considerably over time. He argues, for example, that in capitalist societies the causal influence of relational structures in the totality of social life has become progressively stronger as more and more areas of social life have been removed from normative regulation. At first, this involved, as Marx recognized, a predominantly economic effect that operated through the emergence and consolidation of a sphere of commodified market relations. As these capitalist societies have developed, however, political regulation has become a progressively greater feature of these market relations, and it is a politicized economy that now plays the crucial part in shaping the overall social totality, leading to the commodification and juridification of all human relations. Individuals are increasingly connected to one another through 'delinguistified media' such as money and power. While operating as increasingly autonomous relational structures, these media are, nevertheless, 'anchored' in the life world through the 'institutional complexes' of the legal and administrative systems. These institutional complexes, Habermas argues, are not a 'material base', as Marx held, but are, indeed, the 'basic institutions' or 'core institutions' of capitalist society. The articulation of 'base' and 'superstructure' has been reconstructed and can no longer be grasped in the old language.

It is not necessary to follow Habermas in all the particulars of his account of the development of late capitalism. What is important is the model of social structure that he uses in this account. He has attempted, with much success, to combine the insights of the base/superstructure model and the system/subsystem model. He has not, however, resolved the problems inherent in these two metaphors, taking them on largely as he found them.

Fields and the organization of space

A major problem with Habermas's model is one that – unsurprisingly – is common to many forms of Marxism and systems theory. This is the tendency to see the historical development of social totalities as realizing a goal that is somehow given in the social structure itself. Althusser (1968: 96–7) has criticized this as historicism or teleology. Historicist theories, Althusser holds, conceptualize social structures as 'expressive totalities', as manifesting specific principles that suffuse them and give them their shapes. All levels of a particular social structure express this essential principle, and this manifests itself ever more clearly as the structure develops. For example, Marx tended to see the contradiction between capital and labour in capitalist social structures as conditioning all other aspects of the social structure. The entire social structure expresses this same contradiction.

Althusser sought to replace the idea of an expressive totality with that of social structure as a 'complexly articulated whole' in which each level has its 'relative autonomy'. The various levels are connected with and influence one another; they are 'overdetermined', but they do not follow a single developmental logic. The contradictions that exist within systems of economic relations and institutions, for example, are unlikely to be the same as those that are found in cultural or political systems. The various contradictions will not, therefore, reinforce one another and there will be no consistent drive in any one direction of social change. Althusser argued that it is only when contradictions at different structural levels do happen to align themselves, reinforcing each other's effects, that there will be a 'fusion' or 'condensation' of social forces that will create a tendency towards wholesale structural transformation. If, on the other hand, the contradictions do not align themselves then there will be a 'displacement' of contradictions (Althusser 1963: 210–13).

Althusser struggled to find a language that would adequately grasp this view of social structure. He saw it as involving what he called 'structural causality', a mechanism through which 'the whole existence of the structure consists of its effects' (Althusser and Balibar 1968: 189). A social structure, he said, is a 'decentred structure in dominance'. Each level of social structure follows its own eccentric course, subject only to the need to adapt to all others, and, within this articulation of structures, one particular level has the greatest effect (Althusser 1962: 254–5). Following Marx, Althusser saw economic relations as having the greatest influence on the overall direction of social development. He argued that this is very different from the fundamental or essential role of a determining economic base. A social structure as a whole is an effect of the *simultaneous*, and complex, articulation of different relations and institutions. The metaphor that Althusser most consistently relied on is that of the electric or magnetic field. It is the combination of different forces in a field that gives objects their properties. Objects are not entities that exist prior to or separate from the existence of forces in social fields; they are constituted through these forces.[6]

This decentring of social structures – and of the subject – removes the idea of essence from structural analysis, and it has been taken further in the so-called post-structuralist ideas of Foucault and in the writings of Bourdieu. While rejecting the idea of 'structure' that is found in much structuralist writing, Foucault does not completely reject the possibility of a concept of structure or social organization. He certainly tends to avoid the word, because of some of the connotations that it inherits from earlier traditions of social thought, but his work does embody an attempt to elaborate on the differentiated, fragmented and eccentric characteristics of social structures to which Althusser pointed.

Foucault (1971) saw knowledge and ideas (discourse) as both constitutive of and produced by social development. This process of social development is not continuous, linear and progressive, but is organized around significant discontinuities and ruptures.[7] A form of social organization, like the bodies of knowledge that are integral to it, is to be understood as a 'system of dispersion' (Foucault: 38) that must be understood as a network or 'archipelago' of autonomous elements.

As Major-Poetzl (1983) has convincingly argued, Foucault conceives of social space along the lines of post-Newtonian field physics, and he systematically employs spatio-temporal categories.[8] In field physics, objects are not primary or simply given; they are the relational and contingent results of the organization of space as a field. Moreover, they are rarely the results of a single, homogeneous effect, but tend to arise from distinct localized 'surfaces of emergence', such as hospitals, asylums, and prisons. Social structure is conceptualized as the effect of dynamic and dispersed configurations of institutional and relational structures in a fractured and heterogeneous social space.

This recognition of contingency, rupture and discontinuity does not itself mean the abandonment of the attempt to conceptualize complexly articulated levels of social structure. This is clear from the way that Bourdieu has built on these ideas. Bourdieu insists that sociology must rid itself of all 'substantialist concepts' that suggest the existence of things independently of the relations that constitute them.

The concept of space is a crucial starting point for producing theoretical representations of society, because '. . . social space is indeed the first and last reality' (Bourdieu 1994: 13). The idea of space impels us towards a relational understanding of the world:

> It affirms that every 'reality' it designates resides in the mutual exteriority of its composite elements. Apparent, directly visible beings, whether individuals or groups, exist and subsist in and through difference; that is, they occupy relative positions in a space of relations which, although invisible and always difficult to show empirically, is the most real reality . . . and the real principle of the behaviour of individuals and groups.
>
> (Bourdieu 1994: 31)

Social space is not merely an aggregate of individuals. It is, as we will show in Chapter 6, a distribution of resources and embodied practices or dispositions into different social positions. The positions themselves exist only in their opposition and difference to other positions. These may be institutional or relational positions as we have described them in Chapters 3 and 4. Thus, the position of man is opposed to that of woman, of good taste to bad taste, of high art to popular art, of educated to uneducated, and so on. Social space as a whole is organized into a number of different fields of activity, and positions in one field may be related to positions in other fields through similarity or homology. Thus, a homology or equivalence may exist between positions in relation to education and the socially positioned practices of good taste and knowledge of high art (Bourdieu 1984: 175).

Bourdieu has pointed to a variety of different fields that exist in societies, and he has himself undertaken studies of the fields of taste (Bourdieu 1986), academic and intellectual production (Bourdieu 1988), artistic creation (Bourdieu 1984: 139–48; 1993b), education (Bourdieu and Passeron 1970), language (Bourdieu 1991) and the bureaucratic state (Bourdieu 1989). A society – as a social space – consists of a multiplicity of fields in complex articulations with one another. They are not simply 'nested' one inside another, as are the Parsonian systems and subsystems, but may overlap and intersect, interfering with or reinforcing each other's effects.

While the range and character of social fields is immense, Bourdieu holds that it is possible to identify certain general features in them (1984: 72). Fields are 'arenas of struggle' over the possession and reproduction of the resources that are specific to them. These resources – Bourdieu calls them forms of 'capital' – are modalities of social power. They are distributed unevenly among the various positions in a field, and they are the bases for relations of domination and subordination and for struggles over dominance within a field (Bourdieu 1994: 31). Those who occupy social positions that give them advantaged access to resources are able to dominate the field, and reap the rewards that it has to offer. At the most general level, Bourdieu makes a distinction between four different types of resource, which he calls economic, cultural, social, and, at a slightly different level, symbolic. The economic field, for example, involves the distribution of and struggle over such resources as income, land, and financial assets as means to the securing of profit.

Bourdieu has undertaken some explorations into the relationship between economic and other types of resources. For example, he has looked at how economic capital can be converted into cultural or educational capital (Bourdieu 1994: 19–30). He has not, however, been interested in examining the economic field itself. This task, he has said, is one that he leaves to others, as his own interests concern cultural and social capital (Bourdieu 1984: 32). Economic resources, as Marx showed, become economic capital when they can be accumulated and invested for the further accumulation of profit.

Cultural resources are various types of symbolic goods, such as language, manners, taste, knowledge and skills. They can be seen as related to the building of institutional structures. These cultural resources can be described as 'capital' when – as is the case with economic resources – it is possible to use them to make cultural 'profits' that can be accumulated and converted into other forms of capital. In a field of cultural consumption, for example, the possession of 'good taste' – as defined by the normative standards that define high status – allows those who possess it to distinguish themselves from those who have 'bad taste'. They can discriminate between artistic and kitsch pictures, fashionable and unfashionable clothes, a good film and a Hollywood blockbuster, artistic and popular music, etc., and they can invest this ability to advantage themselves in organizations, such as schools, that reward the exercise of cultural capital. Holders of cultural capital, then, can accrue the profit inherent in social distinction (Bourdieu 1979). In the field of education, for example, students with the specifically linguistic form of cultural capital have the capacity to express themselves according to the highly valued, socially acceptable standards of their teachers. They will, therefore, profit by being thought of as articulate, bright, and cultured, and will tend to receive the numerous benefits that follow from this (Bourdieu and Passeron 1970. See also Bernstein 1965 and 1971).

'Social capital' is the term that Bourdieu uses to refer to membership in social groups that can enhance a person's opportunities for recruitment, promotion, and mobility into highly valued positions. The relational structures that establish marriage and kinship relations, school and university cliques, attendance at particular colleges, and membership of select clubs can all be employed in this way – in the manner of an 'old boy network' – and they can be converted into cultural or economic capital. Not surprisingly the domestic field of wealthy and powerful families is one of the main bases for the accumulation of social capital (Bourdieu 1994: 71). The fourth type of capital, symbolic capital, is best dealt with in our discussion of embodied structures in the next chapter.

Bourdieu argues that societies like the United States, Japan, and France are fundamentally organized around the distribution of economic and cultural capital. Forms of social capital play a secondary but still important role. Those individuals or groups that are positioned in such a way that they have advantaged access to economic and/or cultural capital are in positions of dominance not only over other individuals or groups in the particular field but in the larger society. Bourdieu refers to this as the overall volume of capital.

A fundamental consequence of the uneven distribution of capital within any field is that there is always an organization of 'interests' and 'stakes', and the conflict of interests is the driving dynamic behind the development of a field. The specific features of the conflict of interests, Bourdieu argues, differ from one field to another, giving each field its specific dynamic – Bourdieu terms it the specific 'logic' of the field. The specific logic of a field is the basis for its autonomy within the overall social space; and the structure of the social space is a result of the interplay of these autonomous logics.

This is not to say that a social space is merely a fragmented aggregate of separate fields. Each field must accommodate to the pressures and strains of coexisting with other fields, and fields are involved in complex interchanges involving the conversion, and reconversion, of one form of capital into another.

Bourdieu maintains that it is also possible to understand the relationships of autonomy and dependence among fields, in terms of their formation into a definite hierarchy. In other words, it is always possible to identify fields that are dominant in particular social formations (Bourdieu 1994: 34). In contemporary France, he holds, cultural capital is dominated by economic capital, but there is no necessary reason why economic capital should always dominate in this way. In the GDR and other Communist societies, for example, the dominant position was taken by the contacts and connections that make up political capital (Bourdieu 1984: 19–30).

As with our discussion of Marx and Parsons, our concern is not with the substantive ideas that Foucault and Bourdieu have set out. We are interested in the underlying method that they use to conceptualize social structures and their levels. Marx's base/superstructure model saw social structures as layered into levels that lie above and below one another, much as the floors of a building rise to various levels above its foundations. The model of systems and subsystems set out by Parsons and other functionalists saw social structures as nested within one another, like the rings of an onion or a Russian Babushka doll. Where Marx's physical imagery stressed the 'vertical' depth of the social, Parsons's imagery moved sociological analysis towards an awareness of its 'lateral' depth. The concept of the field follows Parsons's move away from the misleading physical imagery of the base/superstructure model, but it breaks also with any idea of a simple one-dimensional nesting of subsystems (see Figure 5.3).

A whole society, from this point of view, is a social space within

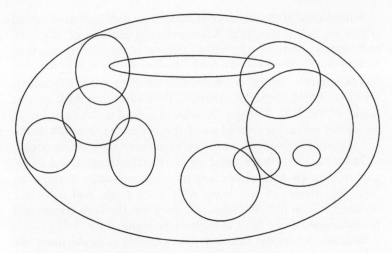

Figure 5.3   Ontological depth: fields and space

which a number of overlapping and interpenetrating fields of action
coexist and follow their own specific developmental dynamics. The
way in which each field develops, however, is affected by the other
fields within the surrounding social space that impinge on its operations, and the operations of each field, therefore, may be rein-
forced by the operations of the others. Within this dispersed space
of autonomous and interpenetrating fields, social structures are
formed that are, themselves, dispersed, discrete, and interpenetrating. The social structures of a society form, in Foucault's words,
an archipelago, a cluster of connected areas of stability and order
that, through their continually shifting relations of interdependence, transform themselves and the overall shape of the archipelago.

   We are not, of course, claiming that Foucault and Bourdieu have
solved the problem of representing social depth or of relating relational to institutional structure; many problems remain. Nonetheless, their work does point to some interesting solutions. The idea
of 'social space', contained in the concept of 'social fields', however,
points to yet another dimension of social structure which is central
to the work of both Foucault and Bourdieu. This is the idea of
embodied structure, which has also been developed, in various
ways, by others. In the next chapter, we will examine some of these
conceptions.

6
Embodied Structure

We have argued that social structures must be seen as having institutional and relational elements. While each aspect of social structure has tended to be explored within different theoretical traditions, neither can properly be understood without the other. However, even a combined account of both the institutional and the relational aspects does not exhaust all that is implied in the concept of social structure. This can be glimpsed in the frequently cited claim that Parsons's concept of institutional structure fails to give an adequate account of how norms come to be enacted. Although he makes great use of a Freudian theory of socialization, his view of social structure tends to assume that norms are consciously understood and unproblematically applied in everyday situations. It is assumed that individuals know which norms are relevant in any particular situation and that they are able simply to implement them in conforming actions.

But things are not this simple. The institutional structure of a society is a virtual order, knowledge of which is distributed among the minds of its individual members. This distribution of knowledge, however, is partial and incomplete. Although individuals may be able to formulate some of the norms that comprise their social institutions, these do not form the actual motives for their actions. Individuals do not typically follow, as a script, the explicit and codified norms that they use to describe their social institutions when they are asked to account for the social practices of their society.

It was considerations such as this that led the symbolic interactionist Herbert Blumer (1962) to argue that sociological analysis would be best served if it abandoned institutional analysis and the functionalism that went with it. Sociology should concentrate instead, he argued, on how individuals negotiate and create the meanings that orientate them in their interactions. In a more radical vein, the ethnomethodologist Aaron Cicourel (1972) argued that sociological analysis had to be concerned with the 'interpretative procedures' that individuals use to make sense of specific inter- actional situations and without which communication would be impossible.

While some of the more radical critics saw a focus on negotiated meanings and interpretative procedures as an alternative to con- ventional sociology, their arguments can also be read as pointing to an additional factor that is necessary if models of institutional and relational structure are to be used. This additional factor has been best understood in the more recent works of Giddens, Foucault, and Bourdieu, all of whom focus, in different ways, on what we have called 'embodied structures'. They have shown that relational and institutional structures are grounded in the situated responses that people make on the basis of the knowledge available to them. This knowledge does not consist of discrete sets of 'facts' and 'ideas', but is a practical competence or ability that is structured into bodily dispositions of action and that generates normatively regulated social actions.

There is another dimension, then, to the ontological depth of social structure, and this dimension is inscribed into human bodies and their ways of thinking, feeling, and behaving as a result of their location in *social space*. From this point of view, the body and bodily presence become central to the production, reproduction, and transformation of social structures. The virtual orders of insti- tutions and relations are 'embodied' in the human organisms whose actions allow us to infer their existence.

Sociology and the body

Durkheim, it will be recalled, saw the collective consciousness as a shared set of ways of thinking, feeling, and behaving, and the point that we are making is that the collective conscience and other aspects of institutional and relational structure can be fully under- stood only if combined with an understanding of embodied struc- tures. While there have been many allusions to the importance of the body – from Marx's emphasis on 'sensual activity' to Parsons's concept of the 'behavioural organism', few of these have provided useful accounts (see, however, Mauss 1935).

For instance, in an analytical review of the development of work on the sociology of the body, Frank has posed an intriguing question. Noting that Mead's well-known statement of symbolic interactionism had been entitled *Mind, Self, and Society*, he asked, 'How would the course of sociology have run differently if Mead's . . . classic work had been titled "Body, Self, and Society"?' (Frank 1991: 36). In his discussion of the ways in which children become socialized as members of social communities (1927: 151–64), Mead, after all, used the concepts of 'play' and 'game', with all the connotations of bodily involvement that this presupposes, and his account of communication focused on the role of the 'gesture', but he did not directly explore the role of the body in interaction. The suggestiveness of Frank's question is further highlighted by the fact that Mead understood the development of human society, and conscious human communication, as 'an end of the process of organic evolution' (Mead 1927: 252). He saw social interaction as rooted in the 'socio-physiological' conditions that permitted individuals to be aware of themselves through the mediation of others, and to adjust their behaviour accordingly (Mead 1927: 253).

Mead was particularly concerned with the processes through which a self develops on the basis of an awareness of social roles. As a result, he understood social interaction primarily in terms of conscious, subjective communication. When Mead wrote about the 'organism', it was usually in terms of the 'physiological system of the human individual's central nervous system' which he rightly saw as integral to communication (p. 255). Thus, Mead held that 'The body is not a self, as such; it becomes a self only when it has developed a mind in the context of social experience' (p. 50). Notwithstanding Mead's hinting at the importance of the body for social communication and organization, then, he ultimately subordinated it to conscious symbolic communication. Face-to-face interaction is seen as mind-to-mind interaction.

Mead's treatment of the body is in some sense paradigmatic of sociology's treatment of the body until quite recently. Thus, to a certain extent, the body has had a 'secret history' (Turner 1991: 12), or has been an 'absent presence' (Shilling 1993: 19) in sociological discourse. We will not be concerned here with the wider debates concerned with the development of a sociology of the body (see Turner 1996, Featherstone *et al.* 1991; Shilling 1993); however it is worth highlighting that the current emphasis on the need for a sociology of the body, and for theories of embodiment, is largely due to the compelling arguments of second-wave feminism, which has sought to bring issues regarding reproductive control, abortion rights and men's control over women's sexuality through violence and pornography into the conceptualization of patriarchy.

Perhaps the most well known, and most problematic, statement of this position is to be found in Shulaminth Firestone's *The Dialectic of Sex*, where she argues that patriarchy is rooted in the biological difference between women and men. That is to say, women reproduce and men do not (Firestone 1971). Firestone's position, however, has been criticized for its inherent biological reductionism. Thus Walby (1990) has argued that control over female reproduction and sexuality is but one of the components in the articulation of a multidimensional understanding of patriarchy that must incorporate a relational and institutional understanding of social structure.

Similarly, Sawicki, drawing on the work of Foucault, has maintained that embodiment and gender identity have to be understood as the result of the location of social practices in fields of social relations (Sawicki 1991: 41–2). Thus, 'the materiality of the body is significant only insofar as it is invested in historically specific ways' (Sawicki 1991: 62). Different types of bodily behaviour, such as gestures, postures, and movements, as well as such activities as dieting, dressing and 'good skin-care habits' (Bartky 1997) are patriarchal forms of embodiment that arise at the intersection of institutional and relational structures. The body, then, is not just a site for the inscription of cultural codes, but also a site of gendered social control (Bordo 1997: 90–1; see also Connell 1987; Butler 1990; Shilling 1993 and Conboy *et al.* 1997).

These lines of argument are generally consistent with the approach to social structure that we have been developing. Instead of seeing *institutional*, *relational* and now *embodied* structure as mutually exclusive conceptions of social structure, we have argued for the possibility of integrating them in order to obtain a more robust conceptualization of the basis of social order. Consequently, in this chapter, we will continue exploring different attempts at theoretically representing the relational and institutional features of social structure in embodied practices.[1]

In the next section we will explore this issue by examining how Giddens draws on both ethnomethodology and Goffman's interactionist model in order to theorize embodied structures. Following this we will turn to two theorists, Foucault and Bourdieu, whose work has decisively put the question of embodied structure on the sociological agenda.

Rules, procedures and structures

In the work of ethnomethodologists such as Garfinkel (1967), Cicourel (1972), and Sacks (1965–72) is found a concern to use the idea of rules to understand social organization. Drawing on Schutz's (1932) phenomenology of action, they have developed a model of social interaction that sees meaning and social life as the achievement of rule-using agents. Cicourel, for example, argued that an explanation of social order in terms of social norms invokes only the 'surface rules' of social life (Cicourel 1970: 27). It is necessary, he argues, to invoke the deeper structure of rules that make such accounts possible.

This argument rests on an analogy with Chomsky's (1957, 1965) method in structural linguistics. This distinguished between the 'linguistic performance' of speech and the deep structure that constitutes 'linguistic competence'. The ability of agents to produce well-formed speech acts depends upon their possessing an inbuilt grammatical competence. Chomsky saw linguistic competence as structures of phonological, semantic and syntactical rules. Although individuals use these rules in their communication with each other, they are generally unaware of them. We speak grammatically, but only professional linguists have any real ability to spell out even the most common of rules that are involved in the production of speech.

Cicourel believed that Chomsky's understanding of language could provide a model for understanding the 'grammar' of social interaction. On this basis, he distinguished the surface structure of norms and social institutions from the deep structure of 'interpretative procedures' that actors draw upon to make sense of each other's actions. Where Chomsky saw grammatical competence as an innate human capacity – an assumption that has been widely questioned – Cicourel stressed that this deep 'sense of social structure' is acquired through social learning. Socialization, however, is not understood in Parsonian terms. It does not involve the acquisition of norms that remain conscious and are consciously applied by actors. It involves, rather, the acquisition of cognitive schemes of which individuals are only partly and imperfectly aware. They learn dispositions to act in patterned ways without consciously having to formulate projects to act in these ways. These procedural rules are the programmes – the mental order – that allow people to act appropriately in the eyes of others and so allow these actions to be reconstructed as being in accordance with institutional norms. They 'activate short and long-term stored information (social distributed knowledge) that enables the actor to articulate general normative rules with immediate interaction scenes' (Cicourel 1968: 40). In so far as social structure exists at all, Cicourel argued, it exists only in the unconscious rules and procedures that individuals deploy in order to make sense of social situations and to produce coordinated actions.

Cicourel's account, like Mead's, concentrated on the development of a sociology of the mind, and he has not pushed this into a broader understanding of the embodiment of social structures. Over a number of years, however, Anthony Giddens has drawn on a similar corpus of ideas and has outlined a more comprehensive sociology of 'embodiment'. One of the difficulties identified in Giddens's discussion of social structure is that he has used the term in a way that is quite at odds with how it has conventionally been used in sociology. For Giddens, social structures are not simply configurations of relations or institutional clusterings, though he accepts that there is some value in continuing to describe them as structures. He stresses, rather, the systems of rules and resources that actors employ in producing these relational and institutional patterns.

Using the linguistic ideas of Saussure, Giddens distinguishes between speech (*parole*) and tongue (*langue*) as a basis for distinguishing between social action and social structure. He argues that action and interaction, like speech, form a socially and temporally situated flow of activity. Social structure on the other hand, like a tongue, does not exist in space or time (Giddens 1976: 125–6). As we have emphasized in earlier chapters, structures have only a 'virtual' existence. Social structure for Giddens consists of the rules, or systems of rules, that give rise to discernible patterns of interaction. They exist only to the extent that they are 'instantiated' or deployed by individuals in their interactions, but they are not reducible to these interactions.

In this sense, Giddens is clearly attempting to overcome the problematic formulation of this issue as it was developed in the work of Erving Goffman. Goffman argued that it was an error to reduce 'all macrosociological features of society . . . to interactional effects' (Goffman 1983: 8), suggesting that we should focus on the 'loose coupling . . . between interactional practices and social structures' (p. 11). Immediately after saying this, however, he argues that the recognition that interactional activity relies on 'matters outside of interaction . . . doesn't in itself imply dependency on social structures' (p. 12). Thus, although he posits the existence of an 'institutional order' that shapes the relational, interactional order, he reveals little about how one might conceptualize its functioning, or how one might go about analysing it.[2]

In Giddens's formulation, structures of rules, like the deep structures of languages, are generative: a grammar provides us with different types of rules for speaking and for generating sentences with meaning, but the grammar is not the speech itself.[3] Giddens sees the practices of individual and collective actors as the means through which they both reproduce and transform the conditions under which they act. These practices are shaped by the institutional and relational structures that both enable and constrain them, but they also invoke the very rules whose use generates these structures. This duality found in structures of rules is the means through which Giddens seeks to overcome the long-standing analytical opposition between a stress on voluntaristic agency and one on deterministic systems (1984). Thus, societies and individuals are mutually interdependent in the social structures that organize practices: '. . . social structure is both constituted by human agency and yet is at the same time the very medium of this constitution' (Giddens 1976: 128–9).

Methodologically, Giddens believes that it is possible to analytically 'bracket' one or other of these two facets of structured practices. Thus, it is possible to examine interaction processes as forms of more or less 'strategic action' and as involving varying degrees of 'social integration', but this can be done only if the specifically systemic features studied in 'institutional analysis' are temporarily left to one side. Similarly, these systemic features can be studied only if there is a shift of attention away from the analysis of strategic conduct. Such methodological bracketing is essential for sociological analysis. Notwithstanding the potential for transformation that is inherent in the reproduction of social structure, Giddens argues that institutional analyses tend to show that social systems remain relatively patterned and orderly. Social institutions – and configurations of relations – are relatively sedimented practices that persist across time and space.

Giddens distinguishes between three aspects of social inter-action, to which specific systemic properties correspond. These are communication, power and morality (Giddens 1976: 129–30). Com-munication, or the mutual understanding of actors through which meanings are constructed and negotiated, is associated with 'symbolic orders' and is structured by the common interpretative schemes that Giddens calls 'structures of signification' or 'semantic codes'. In the same way, the making of moral judgements in inter-action is associated with customs and laws that are structured by moral or legitimation rules. Finally, power is the means through which interacting individuals are able to affect the conduct of others and is associated with economic and political institutions that are structured through authoritative and allocative rules of resource distribution (Giddens 1981).

Actors are generally only partially aware of the rules that are involved in their actions. Indeed, the language of 'rules' is a little misleading, as it would be more accurate to say that actions are undertaken in terms of 'procedures' that are coded into individual memories. They exist as the acquired, embodied skills that organ-ize their actions. Procedural skills are normally exercised in rou-tinized, almost automatic ways. People know *how* to do those things that they have learned, even if they cannot recall this know-ledge to consciousness or codify it in formal language.

One of the features of Giddens's understanding of social struc-ture and its embodiment which allows him to escape the more cog-nitive and mentalisitic connotations to be found in the work of ethnomethodology is his emphasis on the bodily dimension of action and interaction, which he also takes from Goffman's writ-ings. Despite the fact that Goffman's work does not really help us to understand institutional and relational structures, his account of the 'interactional order' does contain an explicit awareness of the role of bodily dispositions in producing them (Turner 1991: 11). Goffman's actors are not disembodied minds; they are corporeal beings that interact in determinate, and often bounded, physical spaces:

> The physical background has certain properties consequent on con-vention and practice. Walls, ceiling and floor tend to establish outside limits to a surround, the assumption being that these barriers are stout enough to keep out potential matters for alarm. They establish an 'inside' and an 'outside'.
>
> (Goffman 1963a: 285)

Goffman's (1959) account of self-presentation explored physicality by seeing social interaction in terms of a 'front' and 'back' region and corresponding public and private spaces. Moreover, corporeal agents are also canvasses on which all manner of social markings are projected. They are 'embodied indicators of status and character' (Goffman 1983: 8) that can be 'read' by other actors. These indicators can signify normality (Goffman 1963a: 238–333), but through the categorization of individuals in terms of supposed 'physical deformities', 'defective characters', or differences of race, nationality or religion, they can also signify 'stigma' and deviance (Goffman 1963b).

The social legitimacy of the performance of 'roles', 'parts' and 'routines' is in part dependent on the performer's bodily bearing and demeanour. Actors do not merely manage the verbal contents of their communications, they demonstrate their social competence by also managing the 'impressions' that they seek to present to their audiences. Thus, for Goffman, '. . . it is social situations that provide the natural theatre in which all bodily displays are enacted and in which all bodily displays are read' (Goffman 1983: 4).

Giddens's development of the concept of practice in terms of the instantiation of rules is meant to incorporate this facet of Goffman's interaction order while linking it to wider features of systemic organization. Thus if Giddens's theory of the embodiment of social structure is to be successful in overcoming the limitation inherent in Goffman's formulation, *structuration theory* must provide a defensible account of the systemic features of social organization.

However, many commentators (for instance Scott 1995: 214) have commented that Giddens's analysis of the systemic moment of the duality of structure remains underdeveloped. In principle Giddens's theory of structuration should be capable of dealing not only with order in interaction but also the principles of order in systems of relations and institutions. Craib (1992: 157–65) has suggested that we can find four ways in which Giddens could account for the structured nature of institutions while still maintaining that the social system itself is not a separate and autonomous structure. One is by seeing institutions as the aggregate effect of structured practices; another is through the routinization of practices, that is to say, the more or less constant repetition of practices in time and space. A third possibility is through the reflexive monitoring of unintended consequences such that individuals adjust their practices so as to preserve a sense of order. Finally, there is the structuring effect of practices on time and space. Craib argues that none of these four possibilities is satisfactory. Moreover, the closer that Giddens gets to providing a more or less convincing answer to the question of the basis of social organization at the level of the social system, the less work his structuration theory seems to do. For instance, agency and individuals virtually disappear from Giddens's historical account of the development of modernity (Giddens 1990).[4]

Bodies, powers and structures

We have shown that Goffman and Giddens have, from different starting points, tried to develop an understanding of the part played by learned bodily dispositions in the reproduction and transformation of social structures. In Giddens, in particular, a concept of embodied structure – of embodied systems of rules or procedures – was set out as a solution to the misleading dualism of agency and system. This idea, however, remains poorly developed, and its specifically bodily dimensions are only weakly formulated. A more comprehensive account of the social structuring of human bodies has been set out by Foucault, and the extensions to this made by Bourdieu connect his work with both Giddens and the earlier writers on institutional and relational structure. For both Foucault and Bourdieu, bodies are seen as the carriers of relational and institutional structures.[5]

Turner (1996: 161) has correctly pointed out that there are two predominant themes running through Foucault's work. On the one hand, there is a concern with the ways that individual bodies become invested with social relations and social institutions. On the other hand, there is a concern with the ways that the control of 'social bodies' – human populations – becomes the major organizational principle of 'modern' societies.[6] Foucault (1961), most famously, sketched the ways in which modern conceptions of madness emerged and how this also involved a parallel concern for the 'health' of social bodies. This concern for the social body gave birth to new regimes and strategies of separation and containment as well as the experts (psychiatrists) and organizations (asylums) able to bring this about. This same concern led to the development of modern medicine (Foucault 1963), educational organizations, armies, factories, and prisons (Foucault 1975), to the disciplining of sexuality (Foucault 1976), and to the establishment of new forms of government (Foucault 1978: 102).[7]

Foucault's treatment of the body and the forms of discipline with which it is invested is an integral part of his account of the organization and distribution of human populations. Individuals are constituted through their location in the organization and distribution of human populations. They gain a sense of themselves, and of appropriate behaviour, because their very bodily activities are regulated by processes of social distribution. Thus the timetable, the temporal elaboration of the act, the correlation of the body and gesture, the relationship between the body and surrounding objects, and the exhaustive use of the body become crucial activities in the spatio-temporal sites where both a body and a sense of self are developed (Foucault 1975: 149–57).

In a school, for example, a child is subjected to a daily and weekly timetable and an annual cycle of events. Together with the specific place in class assigned to her or him, this determines the correct posture and demeanour to adopt in relation to teachers and other pupils within the school. It specifies a need to control writing instruments, play musical instruments, and participate in school games. Movements in and around the school are regulated by clock time, the timetable, the hierarchy of classes, and, perhaps, by gender and ethnicity. Such movements may be physically regulated through the use of bells and whistles, as well as through systems of reward and punishment. The successful disciplining of children's bodies in schools – and their differentiation by class, gender, and ethnicity – allows them to play the parts designated for them in other social structures outside the school. They acquire habits of action that fit them for the places that they occupy, and that they will occupy, in their society.

For this reason, the conformity of individuals to social expectations does not simply originate in their conscious knowledge of norms. It derives from the disciplining power that constitutes individuals by spatially distributing them and organizing and regimenting their activities. The type of power that Foucault associates with this form of organization centred on the distribution of populations is 'bio-power' (Foucault 1975: 202, 1976: 142–3). It is a power that orders the deployment of bodies in social and physical space. As forms of bio-power are connected with forms of knowledge that study, classify and make judgements about the individuals that they discipline, power and knowledge are inextricably linked (Foucault 1976: 98). Such forms of knowledge are differentiated, specialized and socially distributed, meaning that bio-power, too, tends to be dispersed and local in nature. Power relations are mobile, and fluid; they crystallize at the intersection of strategic configurations of social forces in the family, the school, the prison, the workplace, and other social organizations. Foucault does not deny that it is possible to locate major alignments of social power that may provide the basis for large-scale acts of collective resistance. Indeed, Foucault became increasingly interested in examining how 'different micro-powers are invested, realigned and integrated into a global strategy of class domination by the state' (Jessop 1990: 238). For the most part, however, these are 'transitory points of resistance, producing cleavages in a society that shifts about, fracturing unities and effecting regroupings, furrowing across individuals themselves' (Foucault 1976: 96).

Habitus, fields and structures

Foucault's emphasis on dispersal and fluidity in social relations need not be understood, as we showed in Chapter 5, as sounding the death knell for social structure. Quite the opposite, in fact. As Sawicki quite rightly points out, the highlighting of discontinuities is Foucault's starting point and not his ultimate aim (Sawicki 1991: 56–7).The idea of treating institutional and relational structures as spatio-temporal fields of dynamic forces draws attention to the importance of examining the structure of bodily dispositions. Where Foucault has focused attention on the disciplining of bodies, their structuring by social forces, Bourdieu has enlarged on this and has also considered the causal consequences of bodily dispositions for these social forces themselves.

Turner has argued that, whereas the body has been significantly absent from the work of much classical and contemporary sociology, this has not been the case in anthropology (Turner 1991: 1–6). This is perhaps best seen in the work of Mary Douglas who has stressed the ways in which social 'institutions lock into the structure of an analogy from the body' (Douglas 1986: 49). As a result of his own early immersion in anthropology, Bourdieu's writing has consistently emphasized the role of the body as a symbolic carrier of societal norms.

Bourdieu's model of embodiment links bodily dispositions to the positions that individuals occupy in social spaces or fields of activity. As we showed in Chapter 5, he sees that resources are distributed unequally among the various participants in a field, giving each position its specific interests in the acquisition and accumulation of these resources. The norms and social relations that individuals produce, reproduce, and transform in their actions are established in their struggles over these resources. The structure of a social field, like that of a game, depends upon the activities of skilled 'players' who can effectively mobilize their skills. This is not to say that the participants in a field will necessarily have a complete and comprehensive awareness of the conditions under which they act. All that is required, Bourdieu argues, is that individuals develop tendencies to act in one way or another in particular situations. These tendencies can, in fact, be 'infraconscious' and 'infralinguistic' (Bourdieu 1994: 79). That is to say, they may exist below the level of conscious awareness. Tendencies of behaviour are coded into the brain and other organs in such a way that the individuals are able to act in routine ways without having to think consciously about what they ought to be doing.

A simple example can illustrate the general point that Bourdieu is making. Cyclists can ride bicycles without having to give any real thought to the particular movements of arms and legs or to the bodily positions that will maintain their balance. Once they learn to ride a bicycle, their cycling becomes an automated form of behaviour. In the same way, the native speaker of a language can formulate clear and grammatical utterances without having to think about which norms of declension, tense, and number should be applied. Their linguistic competence has provided them with automatic mechanisms for processing their speech. Bourdieu sees such automatic processing as inherent in all routine social activities. Social action is a skilled accomplishment, and human skills of all kinds – skills of cookery, trading, voting, praying, parenting, and so on – are complex, embodied tendencies or dispositions that are acquired through learning and long practice.

It is through the development of such dispositions that the social relations and social institutions of a field come to form what Bourdieu calls 'incorporated capital' (Bourdieu 1980: 56). The objective relations and institutions are incorporated – taken into the corpse or body – as subjective dispositions to act. Values, norms, and ideas, then, come to be fixed in the body as postures, gestures, ways of standing, walking, thinking, and speaking. They are 'embodied social structures' (Bourdieu 1979: 467). That is, they are internalized and generalized expressions of the actual social conditions faced by individuals in their actions. Social conditions are 'internalized and converted into a disposition that generates meaningful practices and meaning-giving perceptions' (1979: 170). In this way, 'morality is made flesh' (Bourdieu 1984: 79), along with structures of thinking and feeling. The whole system of bodily dispositions built up by an individual forms what Bourdieu calls their constitutional 'habitus'.

A habitus is a system of 'durable, transposable dispositions' (1972: 72, emphasis removed), and these dispositions embody quite specific 'generative schemes' (1979: 170). The similarities of action that occur across various fields and that are apparent in their institutional and relational structures are the result of the 'stylistic affinity' that results from the application of such durable schemes to the many novel situations that people face in their everyday lives. Social life is, therefore, organized – and has the appearance of conscious coordination – without there necessarily being any such strategic intention on the part of the individuals involved. Actions may look strategic, despite the fact that they simply follow a 'practical logic'.

These schemes of the habitus operate below the level of consciousness and language, though individuals may, of course, become conscious of them and attempt to formulate them in speech or writing for conscious and deliberate use. Despite this possibility, they operate most typically and most effectively as inbuilt and automatic techniques of the body. This practical reason, or practical belief, is not a state of mind, it is a state of body (Bourdieu 1980: 68). The habitus involves a non-discursive form of 'practical knowledge' that gives a practical 'sense' of what to do and how to do it. In this way, the dispositions of the habitus give people a practical sense of social structure in terms of which they can unreflectively and routinely orientate themselves to one another.

Bourdieu's emphasis on the dispositional character of a habitus neatly avoids the ambiguities that are inherent in Giddens's use of the word 'rules'. The incorporation or embodiment of social structures by individuals does not involve the learning of a set of rules that correspond in a direct and transparent way to institutional norms (Bourdieu 1972: 94–5). A habitus is not a system of coherent rules or deductions from ethical principles. The practical sense of the habitus involves a 'knowledge without concepts' based in generative procedures that regulate without being 'rules' (Bourdieu 1972: 76, 1979: 470).

This does not mean, however, that individuals simply respond mechanically by instinct or rigid habit to outside forces. The operation of a habitus presupposes that individuals make choices, and that their actions are deliberately and creatively organized around the resources of their field of action. Bourdieu's point is that the choices that individuals make are shaped by their habitus, and their habitus is built up from the previous choices that they have made. A habitus organizes the world and the choices available to agents so that they do not need to actively think about it: the 'habitus is spontaneity without consciousness' (Bourdieu 1980: 56). It establishes the unconscious and unacknowledged systems of classification that organize the choices that they make. As a result, choices come to be seen as 'obvious' features of a common-sense and taken-for-granted world.

A habitus develops as children imitate actions and infer patterns that are incorporated as structures that generate their own future actions. In the same way that they infer the grammar of their language, they also infer the cognitive and evaluative codes of kinship, cookery, artistic enjoyment, politics, and so on. Over time, and as they grow older, people modify their habitus – typically without any deliberate intent – as they learn from its application to novel situations. The constraints and opportunities that they experience living in the institutional and relational structures of their society condition their subjectivity and so shape the development of their habitus:

> The habitus acquired in the family underlies the structuring of school experiences . . . , and the habitus transformed by schooling, itself diversified, in turn underlies the structuring of all subsequent experiences (e.g., the reception and assimilation of the messages of the culture industry or work experiences), and so on.
>
> (Bourdieu 1972: 87)

This can be illustrated from Bourdieu's own anthropological fieldwork among the Kabyle people of Algeria. In this work, Bourdieu showed that the relations between women and men depend upon the acquisition of a gender-specific habitus. Cultural values appropriate to each sex make themselves felt, for example, in the learning of particular forms of comportment. Among the Kabyle,

> the specifically feminine virtue, *lah'ia*, modesty, restraint, reserve, orients the whole female body downwards towards the ground, the inside, the house whereas male excellence, *nif*, is asserted in movement upwards, outwards towards other men.
>
> (Bourdieu: 70)

This difference makes itself felt in a variety of contexts. When a

man and a woman gather olives together, the man stands upright
and beats the tree while the woman bends down to collect them.
Similarly, people believe that a man 'should eat with his whole
mouth, wholeheartedly, and not like a woman, just with the lips'
(Bourdieu 1980: 71, 72). In these ways,

> The opposition between male and female is realized in posture, in ges-
> tures and movements of the body, in the form of the opposition
> between the straight and the bent, between firmness, uprightness and
> directness (a man faces forward, looking and striking directly at his
> adversary).
>
> (Bourdieu 1980: 72)

In a similar way, Mary Douglas has shown that the hierarchical
order of the caste system operates through the organization and pro-
hibition of all manner of bodily contacts and exchanges – sexual
contact, physical contact, food preparation, and so on. Consequently, the body not only provides resources for the articulation of
symbolic ideas of purity and danger, it is also one of the principal
sites where social divisions are reproduced (Douglas 1966: 124–8).

Bourdieu does not make the mistake often attributed to Parsons
of assuming a cultural consensus in which socialization produces
identically socialized automata. Societies consist of differentiated
and often contradictory spheres of activity, and quite distinct clusters of dispositions are associated with each of their various social
positions. Inequalities in the various kinds of resources that are distributed throughout a system of fields give rise to power differences
that organize social positions into classes, genders, and a whole
array of specialized social groups and agencies. Specific occupations and fields of activity generate distinct systems of dispositions among their participants, and as each person is a participant
in a number of different social fields, the habitus of any one individual will tend to be quite different from that of another. Our discussion of Bourdieu's Kabyle fieldwork showed that women and
men each tend to have their characteristic habitus, and much of
Bourdieu's other work has explored the formation and significance
of the differentiation of a dominant class habitus from a subordinate class habitus. A class habitus is 'the internalized form of class
condition' (Bourdieu 1979: 101). It is the result of the particular
experiences and opportunities shared by those who occupy a particular class position. It is because people acquire a class-specific
habitus that there are similar patterns of class action in various

fields of activity; and it is because of these similar objective patterns that they acquire the habitus. Politics, leisure, religion, art, and so on all show similar patterns of class behaviour when they are the results of – and therefore the conditions for – the application of class habituses (Bourdieu 1979: 175).

Individuals acquire these systems of classification and social behaviour without realizing that they are doing so. This hides the fact that they depend upon distributions of social power and different types of capital. This is what Bourdieu tries to grasp in his idea of symbolic capital. When the socially acquired dispositions and capital of dominant agents are seen as legitimate, or as having the highest cultural value, they possess a symbolic capital or 'profit of honour' (Bourdieu 1994: 103) over and above the value of their economic and cultural capital. Because the acceptance of this 'distinction' by others depends upon hidden power relations, Bourdieu refers to it as 'symbolic violence'.[8]

Contemporary societies, Bourdieu argues, are principally structured around the distribution of cultural and economic capital. For this reason, the social positions of a society can be mapped according to the total volume of capital associated with them, and the relative contribution of cultural and economic capital to this total volume (Bourdieu 1994: 5). Such a mapping of social positions also shows the habitus associated with each of them. Thus, Bourdieu argues that the habitus of higher education teachers reflects the fact that their high volume of capital is weighted towards the cultural, while the habitus of those in the professions reflects the fact that their similar overall volume of capital is weighted more evenly. Primary school teachers, on the other hand, have the same relative weighting of economic and cultural capital as higher education teachers, but their overall volume of capital is much smaller and their habitus is correspondingly different. Thus, Bourdieu locates embodied structures of class dispositions that correspond to the relational and institutional structures that define the fields of power that comprise any society.

The works that we have discussed in this chapter provide powerful understandings of the embodiment of social structure, but much work remains to be done in developing this idea as clearly and systematically as has happened with the concepts of institutional and relational structure. No less important is the task of continuing to build conceptual and theoretical links among the different facets of social structure that we have examined.

We have tried to set out, as clearly as possible, the ways in which these facets of social structure have been explored and articulated by their most systematic and forceful advocates. This advocacy has sometimes led theorists to shift from advocacy of the importance of one facet of social structure to advocacy of its primacy – and often, then, to advocacy of the idea that social structure consists of nothing other than this facet. A recognition of the interdependence of normative institutions and actual social relations in the work of Parsons, for example, led him to try to theorize the primacy of social institutions and, in much of his work, to accord social relations a purely residual character.

We do not deny that there are important questions of primacy to explore – questions of the relative importance of the various aspects of social structure. Indeed, we devoted Chapter 5 to the various attempts that have been made to build the conceptual machinery necessary to theorize the relationship between various 'levels' of social structure. Nevertheless, we have rejected the assumption that any one facet of social structure must, of necessity, always have causal priority. Our argument has been that the various traditions of structural thinking have provided us with the theoretical tools for exploring the variable and constantly changing articulations of the instrumental, relational, and embodied aspects of social structure.

It is for this reason that we have not tried to set out a new and fully integrated model of social structure. Such a task would be premature, and we have highlighted the many difficulties that lie on the path that leads towards this goal. We regard this book as very much a summary of the current state of play among those who have considered the question of social structure and the part that it plays in social life. We have tried to clear the ground of the confusions and uncertainties that have beset many discussions of the subject. We have tried to set out the views of social structure that are implied in much existing social research and that can help to inform empirical work in the future. Only by being clear about what is meant by 'social structure' is it possible to undertake defensible forms of structural analysis in empirical work.

We hope, however, that our discussion of structural ideas in this book may help in attempts to move beyond existing theorizations of social structure and to move a little further along the path that we have signposted. Such attempts will not, however, be limited to the consideration of 'structural' issues alone. Structural thinking must be developed alongside a consideration of how action and agency are to be understood. Structural analysis has sometimes seemed to be denied by any recognition of the importance of agency, subjectivity, and the narrative forms through which people account for their actions and construct their identities. This is not our view. It has established itself, we hold, because of the failure of practising sociologists to uncover the concepts of social structure that are required in their work, and the corresponding assumption by action theorists that there is, therefore, no such thing as social structure. The time has come to move beyond the sterile opposition of 'structure' and 'action' and the mutual misunderstandings that lie behind it. Both action and structure have their part to play in sociological analysis, and some of the most interesting and important work in sociology today is, at last, beginning the task of establishing a coherent understanding of their relationship. We hope that, in some small way, this book might help to clarify the terms of that debate.

Notes

Chapter 1

1 This does not mean, of course, that the meaning is entirely open and subject to an infinite deferral (Lopez 1999; Potter 1999).

Chapter 2

1 It will become apparent that we completely reject Porpora's (1987) misreading of Durkheim's concept of social structure as any statistical regularity in social life.

2 Durkheim (1898) attempted to distinguish 'individual representations' from collective representations on the grounds that the former were the direct products of the individual brain and its sensory apparatus. This attempt was not wholly successful, but this particular problem is not directly relevant to our concerns here.

Chapter 3

1 During the 1950s, Parsons adopted biologist Alfred Emerson's suggestion that, as a store of coded information, the cultural symbol is analogous to the gene. Parsons held that patterns of culture are analogous to the genetic heritage of an individual. See Emerson (1956) and Parsons and Smelser (Parsons and Bales 1956: 395–9; Parsons 1970). This was many years before Dawkins's (1976) now celebrated suggestion that the cultural 'meme' should be seen as an analogue of the gene.

2 Parsons's visit to the London School of Economics in 1924–5 had exposed him to the influence of Hobhouse (1924) and his teaching assistant, Maurice Ginsberg. These two, and Ginsberg in particular, presented an influential critique of Durkheim's supposed reliance on a

theory of the 'group mind'. Not until the early 1930s did Parsons shake off the influence of this reading of Durkheim (Parsons 1970).

3 Archer, like Popper, emphasizes the logical connections among cultural elements. Whether stylistic and ethical patterns can be reduced, as she suggests, to purely logical patterns is a moot point.

4 Language, however, is not only an example of a particular cultural system. It has also been the basis for 'semiotic' studies of cultural systems in general. Theorists such as Claude Lévi-Strauss and Roland Barthes and, more recently, writers in cultural studies have used this approach to explore a wide range of cultural phenomena. We do not have the space to deal with these here. However, notwithstanding important differences between the Parsonian-inspired, and the more linguistically based understandings of culture, they do converge in stressing the systematic character of cultural objects that are not reducible to the individuals who express themselves through them.

5 Parsons and his school tended to see the absence of norms as resulting in a 'Hobbesian' conflict situation where social action is the biologically driven pursuit of narrow self-interest. In fact, this is not implied by a recognition of the importance of social norms, and the so-called Hobbesian model is inadequate.

6 Exactly the same point had been made some years before by the sociologist Eisenstadt (1965: 22). This was, of course, a development of Durkheim's (1893) remarks on the non-contractual elements in contract.

7 Many writers in the normative functionalist tradition write about 'social status' rather than social position. This misleading terminology is better avoided (see Scott 1996: Chapter 4), and we use the word 'position' throughout this book.

8 Some have attempted to use the concept of role to describe the actual behaviour that is associated with a social position (e.g. Newcomb 1951: 330). However, the logic of the institutionalist argument requires a focus on expected behaviour rather than actual behaviour. The relationship between expected and actual behaviour is a feature of the relationship between institutional and relational structure (Levy 1952: 158–60).

9 Indeed, Banton (1965: 36) has suggested that the concept of position (or 'status', as he terms it) is redundant. It seems important, however, to retain some way of distinguishing the positional and the performative aspects of people's social actions.

10 These substantive claims need not be pursued, as they are not part of his concept of social structure *per se*. Briefly, he sees authority as establishing powers of legitimate command for certain roles and rights of autonomy for others. Status stratification – ranking in terms of socially shared values – establishes a 'scale' in terms of which rewards and resources are allocated. See Scott (1996) for a discussion of this.

Parsons later saw authority and status stratification as 'integrative institutions', which he distinguished from 'situational' and 'instrumental' institutions (Parsons 1945a: 232). Again, these particular suggestions are not essential to our argument.

11 This is discussed more fully in Scott (1996: 96–8).

12 This is, of course, related to the position developed by elite theorists such as Mosca and Pareto. In view of Parsons's close reading of Pareto, it is perhaps surprising that he did not make more of this possibility. The argument suggested here also has parallels with Gramsci's argument on hegemony and counter-hegemony.

13 *Fatalistic* is not Merton's own term, but comes from Durkheim (1897). Merton gives this social type no specific name, referring simply to ritualism and over-conformity. See also Lockwood (1992: Chapter 3).

14 Merton's discussion of anomie developed an account of how the cultural definition of goals and norms was related to a relational structure of opportunity (Merton 1949: 145). Unfortunately, his sophisticated account of this was not pursued by most structural functionalist writers. On the structure of opportunity see Cloward and Ohlin (1960), cited in the following chapter.

15 There is of course the wider claim made by post-colonial and cultural studies writers that sociology itself is implicated in this process of domination (see During 1993 and Wallerstein 1997). This question is beyond the scope of this study, but see McLennan (1998) for a defence of sociology's explanatory role.

Chapter 4

1 The 1940 paper on social structure is the only part of the Chicago lecture series that Radcliffe-Brown himself revised for publication.

2 Nadel studied philosophy and psychology in Vienna and became a student of Malinowski in 1932. His major work was a study of the Nupe of Nigeria (Nadel 1942). In Vienna he had been influenced by the sociometric ideas that we discuss in the following section.

3 In 1917, he published *Basic Questions of Sociology* (Simmel 1917). Throughout this whole period he continued to work on aesthetics, ethics and the philosophy of history, as well as his formal sociology. The bulk of his 1908 book on sociology has been translated as Wolff (1950) and Wolff and Bendix (1955).

4 Our translation differs from that of Small, which does not bring out Simmel's constant use of textile metaphors. Small's translation is in Simmel (1909: 311).

5 The German terms that he used are *Konstellation*, *Konfiguration*, and *Zusammenkettung*.

6 Simmel's term is *Zweierbindung*, or two-bond, but dyad is the usual

translation. His term for the triad is the *Verbindung zu Dreien* or bonding of three.

7 We have simplified some of the labels that they give to these categories. Mannheim (1934–5) saw positive and negative relations (association and dissociation) as based in 'sympathy' and 'antipathy', which are, in turn, the bases of solidaristic and hostile social relations.

8 Quinney (1970) and Taylor *et al.* (1973) developed influential conflict models of the relational factors underpinning legal institutions.

9 The anthropology that Homans drew on was that undertaken by Lloyd Warner and his associates in a series of factory and community studies that employed the ideas of Radcliffe-Brown. See Warner and Lunt (1941) and Roethlisberger and Dickson (1939).

10 See the summary of this in Scott (2000) and the more advanced discussion in Wasserman and Faust (1994).

11 As we noted earlier, there is an ambiguity in many discussions of 'role'. Nadel tried to develop a purely formal, relational concept of role.

12 When analysed in formal terms, Nadel suggested, such an analysis comes close to the formal sociologies outlined by Simmel and von Wiese.

Chapter 5

1 Margaret Archer (1995) builds directly on some of Bhaskar's insights in her account of social systems.

2 There has been much debate among Marxists about which of the two elements of the economic base is the most important. Balibar (1968) highlights the relations of production, while Cohen (1978) gives primacy to the forces of production. For a critique of this position see Roberts (1996: 114–36).

3 This example was often rendered in terms of the contrast between 'phenomenal form' (surface appearance) and 'real relations' (deep structure) by writers drawing on both the structuralist tradition and a realist philosophy of science. See Benton (1977: 164), Bhaskar (1979) and Keat and Urry (1975: 98–100).

4 A variety of Marxist and Marxian-inspired analysts have offered more substantive and theoretically sophisticated models to deal with these questions. See Jessop (1990) for an excellent, comprehensive, and critical overview.

5 The extent to which Habermas is or is not a Marxist thinker is without doubt a contentious issue but need not detain us here. One indicator of this is the fact that Perry Anderson (1976) did not include Habermas in his survey of Western Marxism.

6 See Major-Poetzl (1983) for the development of the metaphor of the field in the work of Canguilhem, Bachelard and Foucault and its impact on French thought.

7 In arguing this way, Foucault was explicitly drawing on the ideas of Bachelard (1937) and Canguilhem (1977). Both authors stressed the ways in which concepts obtained their meanings by their embedding in wider conceptual networks in their work on the development of concepts in the natural sciences. However, although Foucault's archaeology is concerned with analysing the ways in which specific concepts obtain their meanings through their location in wider conceptual fields, its analytical scope, as we shall see below, is far broader.

8 The concept of the field, taken from field physics, has also had a success-ful history in the field of psychology and social psychology (see Mey 1972).

Chapter 6

1 We cannot here deal with the tension between the 'materiality of the body' and the 'social constructionist' approach to embodiment. For a dis-cussion of the need to articulate a middle ground between these two pos-itions see Shilling (1993).

2 It has been argued that symbolic interactionism cannot provide an account of social structure, though such comments invariably refer to large-scale macrostructures (Maines 1977; Plummer 1991: xi–xii).

3 One of the fundamental problems with Giddens's conceptualization of social structures as systems of 'virtually' existing rules is his inclusion of resources as an aspect of structure. However, it is not clear in what ways resources have a 'virtual' existence (Scott 1995: 208). Nonetheless, he makes the important point that resources do not exist outside the social relations and social institutions through which they are constituted as resources.

4 In more recent work Giddens has dealt with the body in more detail (Giddens 1991), although he has been more concerned with examining the relationship between the body and self-identity in high modernity than with developing a systematic account of the embodiment of social structure. However, see Frank (1991) for an attempt to develop a con-ception of agency, based on structuration theory, that takes seriously the role of the body.

5 In this sense, Foucault and Bourdieu's work exemplifies a distinctive tra-dition in French social theory that has been concerned with identifying the social origins of the subjective principles of classification that corre-spond to different forms of social organization. This emphasis is found in Durkheim's (1912) work on the forms of elementary religions, in Durkheim and Mauss's (1903) work on primitive classifications, and also in the work of Lévi-Strauss and Althusser.

6 Dreyfus and Rabinow (1982) have suggested that there is an intellectual break between two periods in Foucault's work. Gutting (1989: 6–7), on the other hand, suggests that this break is non-existent. Our point here is not to argue for the methodological continuity of Foucault's inquiries, as

much as to show that Foucault's metaphor for social organization remained that of field physics throughout his later work. See also Woodiwiss (1998: 26).

7 The so-called 'governmentality' approach (Burchell *et al.* 1991) has opened up a wide-ranging agenda (Barth 1998: 264–5. See also Rose 1989 and Dean 1999). However, much of this work unfortunately focuses on the 'how' of public and private governance, rather than the 'why' (Woodiwiss 1998: 26).

8 This formulation is Bourdieu's way of understanding a dominant ideology or cultural hegemony, and he makes explicit parallels with Althusser's concept of the ideological state apparatuses.

References

Wherever possible sources have been cited in the text by the date of their first publication in the original language. Dates of translations or later editions consulted are given at the end of each bibliography entry.

Abercrombie, N., Turner, B. and Hill, S. (1979) *The Dominant Ideology Thesis*. London: George Allen & Unwin.

Althusser, L. (1962) 'Notes on a materialist theatre' in L. Althusser, *For Marx*. Harmondsworth: Allen Lane, 1965.

Althusser, L. (1963) 'On the materialist dialectic' in L. Althusser, *For Marx*. Harmondsworth: Allen Lane, 1965.

Althusser, L. (1968) 'The object of capital' in L. Althusser and E. Balibar (eds) *Reading Capital*. London: New Left Books.

Althusser, L. (1971) *Lenin and Philosophy and Other Essays*. London: New Left Books.

Althusser, L. and Balibar, E. (1968) *Reading Capital*. London: New Left Books, 1970.

Anderson, P. (1976) *Considerations on Western Marxism*. London: New Left Books.

Appelbaum, R. P. and Henderson, J. (1992) (eds) *States and Development in the Asia Pacific Region*. Beverley Hills, CA: Sage Publications.

Archer, M. S. (1988) *Culture and Agency*. Cambridge: Cambridge University Press.

Archer, M. S. (1995) *Realist Social Theory: The Morphogenetic Approach*. Cambridge: Cambridge University Press.

Bachelard, G. (1937) *L'expérience de l'espace dans la physique contemporaine*. Paris: PUF.

Bachrach, P. and M. S. Baratz (1962) 'The two faces of power' in J. Scott (1994) (ed.) *Power*. London: Routledge.

Balibar, E. (1968) 'Basic concepts of historical materialism' in L. Althusser and E. Balibar (eds) *Reading Capital*. London: New Left Books.

Banton, M. (1965) *Roles: An Introduction to the Study of Social Relations*. London: Tavistock.

Barnes, J. A. (1954) 'Class and committee in a Norwegian island parish', *Human Relations*, 7: 39–58.

Barrett, M. (1980) *Women's Oppression Today*. London: Verso.

Barrett, M. (1988) 'Introduction' in M. Barrett, *Women's Oppression Today,* Revised Edition. London: Verso.

Barth, L. (1998) 'Michel Foucault' in R. Stones (ed.) *Key Sociological Thinkers*. London: Macmillan.

Bartky, S. L. (1997) 'Foucault, femininity, and the modernisation of patriarchal power' in K. Conboy, N. Medina and S. Stanburgh (eds) *Writing on the Body: Female Embodiment and Feminist Theory*. New York, NY: Columbia University Press.

Benedict, R. (1934) *Patterns of Culture*. London: Routledge and Kegan Paul.

Benton, T. (1977) *Philosophical Foundations of the Three Sociologies*. London: Routledge and Kegan Paul.

Berger, P. L. and Luckmann, T. (1966) *The Social Construction of Reality*. Harmondsworth: Allen Lane, 1971.

Berkowitz, S. D. (1982) *An Introduction to Structural Analysis*. Toronto: Butterworths.

Bernstein, B. (1965) 'A socio-linguistic approach to social learning' in B. Bernstein, *Class, Codes and Control*, Volume 1. London: Routledge and Kegan Paul, 1971.

Bernstein, B. (1971) 'A socio-linguistic approach to socialization: with some reference to educability' in B. Bernstein, *Class, Codes and Control*, Volume 1. London: Routledge and Kegan Paul.

Bhaskar, R. (1975) *The Realist Theory of Science*. Leeds: Leeds Books.

Bhaskar, R. (1979) *The Possibility of Naturalism*. Brighton: Harvester.

Bhaskar, R. (1989) *Reclaiming Reality: A Critical Introduction to Contemporary Philosophy*. London: Verso.

Blau, P. M. (1976) 'Parameters of social structure' in P. M. Blau (ed.) *The Study of Social Structure*. London: Open Books.

Blau, P. M. (1977) *Inequality and Heterogeneity: A Primitive Theory of Social Structure*. New York, NY: The Free Press.

Blau, P. and Duncan, O. D. (1967) *The American Occupational Structure*. New York, NY: Wiley.

Blumer, H. (1962) 'Society as symbolic interaction' in A. Rose (ed.) *Human Behaviour and Social Processes*. London: Routledge and Kegan Paul.

Boorman, S. A. and White, H. C. (1976) 'Social structure from multiple networks: II', *American Journal of Sociology*, 81: 1384–446.

Bordo, S. (1997) 'The Body and the reproduction of feminity' in K. Conboy, N. Medina and S. Stanburgh (eds) *Writing on the Body: Female Embodiment and Feminist Theory*. New York, NY: Columbia University Press.

Bott, E. (1955) 'Urban families: conjugal roles and social networks', *Human Relations*, 8: 345–85.

Bott, E. (1956) 'Urban families: the norms of conjugal roles', *Human Relations*, 9.

Bourdieu, P. (1972) *Outline of a Theory of Practice*. Cambridge: Cambridge University Press, 1977.

Bourdieu, P. (1979) *Distinction: A Social Critique of the Judgment of Taste*. London: Routledge, 1984.

Bourdieu, P. (1980) *The Logic of Practice*. Cambridge: Polity Press, 1990.

Bourdieu, P. (1982) *Language and Symbolic Power*. Cambridge: Polity Press, 1991.

Bourdieu, P. (1984) *Homo Academicus*. Cambridge: Polity Press, 1988.

Bourdieu, P. (1984) *Sociology in Question*. London: Sage, 1993.

Bourdieu, P. (1989) *The State Nobility: Elite Schools in the Field of Power*. Cambridge: Polity Press, 1996.

Bourdieu, P. (1993) *The Field of Cultural Production*. Cambridge: Polity Press.

Bourdieu, P. (1994) *Practical Reason*. Cambridge: Polity Press, 1998.

Bourdieu, P. and Passeron, J. (1970) *Reproduction in Education, Society and Culture*. London: Sage.

Buckley, W. (1967) *Sociology and Modern Systems Theory*. Englewood Cliffs, NJ: Prentice-Hall.

Burchell, G., Gordon, C. and Miller, P. (1991) (eds) *The Foucault Effect*. Chicago, IL: University of Chicago Press.

Burt, R. (1992) *Structural Holes*. New York, NY: Cambridge University Press.

Burt, R. S. (1982) *Towards a Structural Theory of Action*. New York, NY: Academic Press.

Butler, J. (1990) *Gender Trouble*. London: Routledge.

Canguilhem, G. (1968) *Etudes d'histoire et de philosophie des sciences*. Extracted in Francoise Delaporte (ed.) *A Vital Rationalist: Selected Writings from George Canguilhem*. New York: Zone Books.

Canguilhem, G. (1977) *La formation du concept de reflex aux XVIIe et XVIIIe Siecle*. Paris: Urin.

Cartwright, D. and Zander, A. (1953) (eds) *Group Dynamics*. London: Tavistock.

Cavan, R. S. (1928) *Suicide*. Chicago: University of Chicago Press.

Chase-Dunn, C. (1989) *Global Formations*. Cambridge, MA: Blackwell.

Chase-Dunn, C. and Podobnik, B. (1999) 'The next world war: world system cycles and trends' in V. Bornschier and C. Chase-Dunn (eds) *The Future of Global Conflict*. Beverley Hills, CA: Sage.

Chomsky, N. (1957) *Syntactic Structures*. The Hague: Mouton.

Chomsky, N. (1965) *Aspects of the Theory of Syntax*. Cambridge, MA: MIT Press.

Cicourel, A. V. (1968) 'The acquisition of social structure: towards a developmental sociology of language and meaning' in A. Cicourel *Cognitive Sociology*. Harmondsworth: Penguin, 1973.

Cicourel, A. V. (1970) 'Generative semantics and the structure of social interaction' in A. Cicourel *Cognitive Sociology*. Harmondsworth: Penguin, 1973.

Cicourel, A. V. (1972) 'Interpretive procedures and normative rules in the negotiation of status and role' in A. Cicourel *Cognitive Sociology*. Harmondsworth: Penguin, 1973.

Cloward, R. and Ohlin, L. (1960) *Delinquency and Opportunity*. New York, NY: The Free Press.

Cohen, G. A. (1978) *Karl Marx's Theory of History: A Defence*. Oxford: Oxford University Press.

Commons, J. R. [1899–1900] *A Sociological View of Sovereignty*. New York, NY: Augustus M. Kelly, 1965.

Commons, J. R. (1924) *The Legal Foundations of Capitalism*. Madison, WI: University of Wisconsin Press, 1968.

Conboy, K., Medina, N., and Stanbury, S. (eds) (1997) *Writing on the Body: Female Embodiment and Feminist Theory*. New York, NY: Columbia University Press.

Connell. R. (1987) *Gender and Power*. Cambridge: Polity Press.

Coser, L. (1956) *The Functions of Social Conflict*. London: Routledge and Kegan Paul.

Dahrendorf, R. (1957) *Class and Class Conflict in an Industrial Society*. London: Routledge and Kegan Paul, 1959.

Dahrendorf, R. (1958) 'Homo sociologicus: on the history, significance, and limits of the category of social role' in R. Dahrendorf, *Essays in the Theory of Society*. London: Routledge and Kegan Paul, 1968.

Davis, K. (1948) *Human Society*. New York, NY: Macmillan.

Dawe, A. (1970) 'The two sociologies', *British Journal of Sociology*, 21: 207–18.

Dawkins, R. (1976) *The Selfish Gene*. Oxford: Oxford University Press.

Dean, M. (1999) *Governmentality*. London: Sage.

Delphy, C. (1977) *The Main Enemy*. London: Women's Research and Resources Centre.

Douglas, M. (1966) *Purity and Danger*. London: Routledge and Kegan Paul.

Douglas, M. (1986) *How Institutions Think*. London: Routledge, 1987.

Downs, A. (1957) *An Economic Theory of Democracy*. New York, NY: Harper and Brothers.

Drake, S. C. and H. B. Cayton (1945) *Black Metropolis*. New York, NY: Harcourt Brace.

Dreyfus, H. and Rabinow, P. (1982) *Michel Foucault: Beyond Structuralism and Hermeneutics*. Chicago, IL: Chicago University Press.

During, S. (1993) *The Cultural Studies Reader*. London: Routledge.

Durkheim, E. (1893) *The Division of Labour in Society*. London: Macmillan, 1984.

Durkheim, E. (1895) *The Rules of the Sociological Method*. London: Macmillan, 1982.

Durkheim, E. (1897) *Suicide: A Study in Sociology*. London: Routledge and Kegan Paul, 1952.

Durkheim, E. (1898) 'Individual and collective representations' in E. Durkheim (1965) *Sociology and Philosophy* edited by D. F. Pocock and J. G. Peristiany. London: Cohen and West.

Durkheim, E. (1912) *Elementary Forms of the Religious Life*. London: George Allen & Unwin, 1915.

Durkheim, E. and Mauss, M. (1903) *Primitive Classification*. London: Cohen and West, 1963.

Dworkin, D. (1997) *Cultural Marxism in Postwar Britain*. Durham: Duke University Press.

Eisenstadt, S. N. (1965) 'The study of processes of institutionalisation, institutional change, and comparative institutions' in S. N. Eisenstadt, *Essays on Comparative Institutions*. New York, NY: Wiley.

Elias, N. (1939) *The Civilizing Process* (translated in two volumes as *The History of Manners* and *State Formation and Civilization*). Oxford: Basil Blackwell, 1978 and 1982.

Elias, N. (1969) *What is Sociology*? London: Hutchinson, 1978.

Emerson, A. E. (1956) 'Homeostasis and the comparison of social structures' in R. Grinker (ed.) *Towards a Unified Theory of Human Behavior*. New York, NY: Basic Books.

Emirbayer, M. (1997) 'Manifesto for a relational sociology', *American Journal of Sociology*, 103(12): 281–317.

Emirbayer, M. and Goodwin, J. (1994) 'Network analysis, culture, and the problem of agency', *American Journal of Sociology*, 99(6): 1411–54.

Emmanuel, A. (1972) *Unequal Exchange*. New York, NY: Monthly Review Press.

Engels, F. (1884) *The Origin of the Family, Private Property, and the State*. New York, NY: International Publishers, 1942.

Engels, F. (1890) 'Letter to Bloch' in K. Marx and F. Engels *Correspondence, 1846–1895*. London: Lawrence and Wishart, 1934.

Featherstone, M., Hepworth, M. and Turner, B. S. (1991) (eds) *The Body: Social Process and Cultural Theory*. London: Sage.

Firestone, S. (1971) *The Dialectic of Sex*. London: Jonathan Cape.

Fletcher, R. (1965) *Human Needs and Social Order*. London: Michael Joseph.

Foucault, M. (1961) *Madness and Civilization*. New York, NY: Vintage Books, 1973.

Foucault, M. (1963) *The Birth of the Clinic*. New York, NY: Vintage Books, 1975.

Foucault, M. (1971) *The Archaeology of Knowledge*. New York, NY: Pantheon, 1972.

Foucault, M. (1975) *Discipline and Punish*. London: Allen Lane, 1977.

Foucault, M. (1976) *The History of Sexuality, Volume 1: An Introduction*. New York, NY: Vintage Books, 1980.

Foucault, M. (1978) 'Governmentality' in F. Burchell, C. Gordon and P. Miller (eds) *The Foucault Effect*. Chicago, IL: University of Chicago Press, 1991.

Frank, A. G. (1969) *Capitalism and Underdevelopment in Latin America*. Harmondsworth: Penguin.

Frank, A. W. (1991) 'For a sociology of the body: an analytical review' in M. Featherstone, M. Hepworth and B. Turner (eds) *The Body: Social Process and Cultural Theory*. London: Sage.

Freeman, L. C. (1983) 'Spheres, cubes, and boxes: graph dimensionality and network structure', *Social Networks*, 5: 139–56.

Garfinkel, H. (1967) *Studies in Ethnomethodology*. New Jersey, NJ: Prentice-Hall.

Geiger, T. (1949) *Die Klassengesellschaft im Schmelztiegel*. Köln: Hagen.

Giddens, A. (1976) *New Rules of the Sociological Method*. London: Hutchinson.

Giddens, A. (1981) *A Contemporary Critique of Historical Materialism, Volume 1: Power, Property and the State*. London: Macmillan.

Giddens, A. (1984) *The Constitution of Society*. Cambridge: Polity Press.

Giddens, A. (1990) *Consequences of Modernity*. Cambridge: Polity Press.

Giddens, A. (1991) *Modernity and Self-Identity*. Cambridge: Polity Press.

Godelier, M. (1984) *The Mental and the Material*. London: Verso.

Goffman, E. (1959) *The Presentation of Self in Everyday Life*. Harmondsworth: Penguin.

Goffman, E. (1963a) *Relations in Public Places*. New York, NY: Free Press.

Goffman, E. (1963b) *Stigma*. Englewood Cliffs, NJ: Prentice-Hall.

Goffman, E. (1983) 'The interaction order', *American Sociological Review*, 48: 1–17.

Gramsci, A. (1929–35) *Prison Notebooks*. London: Lawrence and Wishart, 1971.

Granovetter, M. (1973) 'The strength of weak ties', *American Journal of Sociology*, 78: 1360–80.

Granovetter, M. (1974) *Getting a Job*. Cambridge, MA: Harvard University Press.

Granovetter, M. (1986) 'Economic action and social structure: the problem of embeddedness', *American Journal of Sociology*, 81: 481–510.

Gross, N. W., Mason, S. and Mc Eachern, A. W. (1958) *Explorations in Role Analysis: Studies of the School Superintendency Role*. New York, NY: Wiley.

Grossberg, L., Nelson, C. and Treichler, P. (1992) (eds) *Cultural Studies*. London: Routledge.

Gutting, G. (1989) *Michel Foucault's Archaeology of Scientific Reason.* Cambridge: Cambridge University Press.

Habermas, J. (1981a) *The Theory of Communicative Action, Volume 1.* London: Heinemann, 1984.

Habermas, J. (1981b) *The Theory of Communicative Action, Volume 2.* London: Heinemann, 1987.

Hamilton, G. G. (1984) 'Patriarchalism in Imperial China and Western Europe: a revision of Weber's sociology of domination', *Theory and Society*, 13: 393–425.

Harary, F. and Norman, R. Z. (1953) *Graph Theory as a Mathematical Model in Social Science.* Ann Arbor, MI: Institute for Social Research.

Hartsock, N. (1984) *Money, Sex and Power.* Boston, MA: Northeastern University Press.

Hechter, M. (1975) *Internal Colonialism: The Celtic Fringe in British National Development, 1536–1966.* London: Routledge and Kegan Paul.

Hegel, G. W. F. (1807) *Hegel's Philosophy of Mind [Die Philosophie des Geistes].* Oxford: Oxford University Press, 1971.

Hobhouse, L. T. (1924) *Social Development: Its Nature and Conditions.* London: George Allen & Unwin, 1966.

Holzner, B. (1968) *Reality Construction in Society.* Cambridge, MA: Schenkman.

Homans, G. (1950) *The Human Group.* London: Routledge and Kegan Paul, 1951.

Horkheimer, M., Adorno, T. and the Institute of Social Research (1956) *Aspects of Sociology.* London: Heinemann, 1973.

Jarvie, I. C. (1972) *Concepts and Society.* London: Routledge and Kegan Paul.

Jay, M. (1984) *Marxism and Totality.* Cambridge: Polity Press.

Jessop, B. (1990) *State Theory: Putting the Capitalist State in its Place.* Cambridge: Polity.

Keat, R. and Urry, J. (1975) *Social Theory as Science.* London: Routledge and Kegan Paul.

Kluckhohn, C. (1954) 'Culture and behaviour' in G. Lindzey (ed.) *Handbook of Social Psychology, Volume 2.* Cambridge, MA: Addison-Wesley.

Kroeber, A. (1917) 'The superorganic', *American Anthropologist*, 19: 163–213.

Kroeber, A. and Kluckhohn, C. (1952) *Culture: A Critical Review of Concepts and Definitions.* New York, NY: Vintage Books, 1963.

Larrain, J. (1979) *The Concept of Ideology.* London: Hutchinson.

Laumann, E. O. (1966) *Prestige and Association in an Urban Community.* Indianapolis, IN: Bobbs-Merrill.

Lemert, C. (1997) *Postmodernism is Not What You Think.* Mulden, MA: Blackwell.

Levine, D. (1991) 'Simmel reappraised: old images and new scholarship' in C. Camic (1997) (ed.) *Reading the Sociological Classics*. Oxford: Basil Blackwell.

Lévi-Strauss, C. (1968) *Structural Anthropology*. London: Allen Lane; Penguin.

Levy, M. J. (1952) *The Structure of Society*. New Jersey, NJ: Princeton University Press.

Linton, R. (1936) *The Study of Man*. New York, NY: D. Appleton-Century.

Linton, R. (1945) *The Cultural Background of Personality*. New York, NY: D. Appleton-Century.

Lockwood, D. (1956) 'Some remarks on the social system', *British Journal of Sociology*, 7: 134–46.

Lockwood, D. (1964) 'Social integration and system integration', in G. Zollschan and W. Hirsch (1976) (eds) *Social Change*. New York, NY: John Wiley.

Lockwood, D. (1992) *Solidarity and Schism*. Oxford: Clarendon Press.

López, J. (1999) The Discursive Exigencies of Enunciating the Concept of Social Structure and Five Case Studies – Althusser, Durkheim, Marx, Parsons, Weber. Unpublished PhD thesis, Essex University.

Lorrain, F. and White, H. C. (1971) 'Structural equivalence of individuals in social networks', *Journal of Mathematical Sociology*, 1: 49–80.

Luhmann, N. (1975) 'The differentiation of society' in N. Luhmann *The Differentiation of Society*. New York, NY: Columbia University Press, 1982.

Lukes, S. (1973) *Emile Durkheim: His Life and Work*. Harmondsworth: Allen Lane; Penguin.

McClintock, A., Mufti, A. and Shohat, E. (1997) (eds) *Dangerous Liaisons: Gender, Nation and Postcolonial Perspectives*. Minneapolis, MN and London: University of Minnesota Press.

McDougall, W. (1908) *An Introduction to Social Psychology*. London: Methuen, 1923.

McLennan, G. (1998) 'Sociology and cultural studies: rhetorics of disciplinary identity', *History of the Human Sciences*, 11: 1–17.

Maines, D. R. (1977) 'Social organization and social structure in symbolic interactionist thought', *Annual Review of Sociology*, 3: 235–59.

Major-Poetzl, P. (1983) *Michel Foucault's Archaeology of Western Culture: Toward a New Science of History*. Chapel Hill, NC: University of North Carolina Press.

Mann, M. (1970) 'The social cohesion of liberal democracy', *American Sociological Review*, 35: 423–39.

Mann, M. (1986) *The Sources of Social Power, Volume 1: A History of Power from the Beginning to AD 1760*. Cambridge: Cambridge University Press.

Mannheim, K. (1929) 'Ideology and Utopia', in K. Mannheim *Ideology and Utopia*. London: Routledge and Kegan Paul, 1936.

Mannheim, K. (1934–5) 'Systematic sociology', in K. Mannheim, *Systematic Sociology*. London: Routledge and Kegan Paul, 1957.

March, J. G. and J. P. Olsen (1989) *Rediscovering Institutions: The Organizational Basis of Politics*. New York, NY: The Free Press.

Marsh, D. C. (1961) *The Changing Social Structure of England and Wales*. London: Routledge and Kegan Paul.

Marx, K. (1845) 'Theses on Feuerbach' in E. Kamenka (ed.) (1983) *The Portable Karl Marx*. Harmondsworth: Penguin.

Marx, K. (1852) 'The Eighteenth Brumaire of Louis Bonaparte', in K. Marx and F. Engels (eds) *Selected Works Vol. 1*. London: Lawrence & Wishart, 1968.

Marx, K. (1859) 'A contribution to the critique of political economy: preface' in E. Kamenka (ed.) (1983) *The Portable Karl Marx*. Harmondsworth: Penguin.

Marx, K. and Engels, F. (1846) *The German Ideology*. London: Lawrence and Wishart, 1970.

Marx, K. and Engels, F. (1848) *The Communist Manifesto*. Harmondsworth: Penguin, 1967.

Mauss, M. (1935) 'Techniques of the body', *Economy and Society*, 2: 70–88.

Mead, G. H. (1927) *Mind, Self, and Society from the Standpoint of Social Behaviourism*. Chicago, IL: University of Chicago Press, 1934.

Merton, R. K. (1949) 'Social structure and anomie' in R. K. Merton *Social Theory and Social Structure*, Revised Edition. New York, NY: The Free Press of Glencoe, 1957.

Merton, R. K. (1957a) 'Continuities in the theory of social structure and anomie' in R. K. Merton, *Social Theory and Social Structure,* Revised Edition. New York, NY: The Free Press of Glencoe.

Merton, R. K. (1957b) 'The role set: problems in sociological theory', *British Journal of Sociology*, 8.

Merton, R. K. and Barber, E. (1963) 'Sociological ambivalence' in E. Tiryakian, *Sociological Theory, Values, and Sociocultural Change*. New York, NY: The Free Press.

Mey, H. (1972) *Field Theory in Social Science*. London: Routledge and Kegan Paul.

Meyer, J. W. and Rowan, B. (1977) 'Institutionalized organizations: formal structure as myth and ceremony', *American Journal of Sociology*, 83: 340–63.

Meyer, J. W. and Scott, W. R. (1983) *Organizational Environments: Ritual and Rationality*. Beverley Hills, CA: Sage.

Meyer, J. W., Boli, J., Thomas, G. M. and Ramirez, F. O. (1997) 'World society and the nation-state', *American Journal of Sociology*, 103: 144–81.

Millet, K. (1970) *Sexual Politics*. New York, NY: Doubleday.

Mitchell, J. C. (1969) 'The concept and use of social networks' in J. C. Mitchell (ed.) *Social Networks in Urban Situations*. Manchester: Manchester University Press.

Moreno, J. L. (1934) *Who Shall Survive?* New York, NY: Beacon Press.

Mouzelis, N. (1991) *Sociological Theory: What Went Wrong?* London: Routledge.

Mullins, N. C. (1973) *Theories and Theory Groups in American Sociology*. New York, NY: Harper and Row.

Murdock, G. P. (1949) *Social Structure*. New York, NY: The Free Press.

Murray, M. (1995) *The Law of the Father*. London: Routledge.

Nadel, S. F. (1942) *A Black Byzantium: The Kingdom of Nupe in Nigeria*. London: Oxford University Press.

Nadel, S. F. (1951) *Foundations of Social Anthropology*. London: Cohen and West.

Nadel, S. F. (1957) *The Theory of Social Structure*. Glencoe: The Free Press.

Nelson, R. and Winter, S. (1982) *An Evolutionary Theory of Economic Change*. Cambridge, MA: Harvard University Press.

Newcomb, T. M. (1951) *Social Psychology*. New York, NY: Dryden Press.

North, D. C. (1990) *Institutions, Institutional Change, and Economic Performance*. Cambridge: Cambridge University Press.

Park, R. E. and Burgess, E. W. (1925) *The City*. Chicago, IL: University of Chicago Press, 1967.

Parsons, T. (1937) *The Structure of Social Action*. New York, NY: McGraw-Hill.

Parsons, T. (1940a) 'An analytical approach to the theory of social stratification' in T. Parsons *Essays in Sociological Theory*, Second Edition. New York, NY: The Free Press, 1954.

Parsons, T. (1940b) 'The motivation of economic activity' in T. Parsons *Essays in Sociological Theory*, Second Edition. New York, NY: The Free Press, 1954.

Parsons, T. (1942a) 'Democracy and social structure in pre-Nazi Germany' in T. Parsons *Essays in Sociological Theory*, Second Edition. New York, NY: The Free Press, 1954.

Parsons, T. (1942b) 'Propaganda and social control' in T. Parsons *Essays in Sociological Theory*, Second Edition. New York, NY: The Free Press, 1954.

Parsons, T. (1942c) 'Some sociological aspects of Fascist movements' in T. Parsons *Essays in Sociological Theory*, Second Edition. New York, NY: The Free Press, 1954.

Parsons, T. (1945a) 'The present position and prospects of systematic theory in sociology' in T. Parsons *Essays in Sociological Theory*, Second Edition. New York, NY: The Free Press, 1954.

Parsons, T. (1945b) 'The problem of controlled institutional change' in T. Parsons *Essays in Sociological Theory*, Second Edition. New York, NY: The Free Press, 1954.

Parsons, T. (1951) *The Social System*. New York, NY: The Free Press.

Parsons, T. (1957) 'Malinowski's theory of social systems' in R. Firth (ed.) *Man and Culture*. London: Routledge and Kegan Paul.

Parsons, T. (1960) 'Durkheim's contribution to the theory of the integration of social systems' in T. Parsons, *Sociological Theory and Modern Society*. New York, NY: The Free Press.

Parsons, T. (1966) *Societies: Evolutionary and Comparative Perspectives*. Englewood Cliffs, NJ: Prentice-Hall.

Parsons, T. (1970) 'On building social systems theory' in T. Parsons *Social Systems and the Evolution of Action Theory*. New York, NY: The Free Press, 1977.

Parsons, T. (1971a) 'Comparative Studies and Evolutionary Change' in T. Parsons, *Social Systems and the Evolution of Action Theory*. New York, NY: The Free Press, 1977.

Parsons, T. (1971b) *The System of Modern Societies*. Englewood Cliffs, NJ: Prentice-Hall.

Parsons, T. (1975) 'The present status of structural-functional theory in sociology' in T. Parsons *Social Systems and the Evolution of Action Theory*. New York, NY: The Free Press, 1977.

Parsons, T. and Bales, R. F. (1956) *Family, Socialization and Interaction Process*. London: Routledge and Kegan Paul.

Plummer, K. (1991) 'Introduction: the future of interactionist sociologies' in K. Plummer (ed.) *Symbolic Interactionism, Volume 2*. Aldershot: Edward Elgar.

Popitz, H. (1967) 'The concept of social role as an element of sociological theory' in J. A. Jackson (ed.) *Role*. Cambridge: Cambridge University Press.

Porpora, D. (1987) *The Concept of Social Structure*. Westport, CT: Greenwood Press.

Potter, G. (1999) *The Bet: Truth in Science, Literature and Everyday Knowledges*. Aldershot: Ashgate.

Powell, W. W. and Di Maggio, J. (eds) (1991) *The New Institutionalism in Organizational Analysis*. Chicago, IL: University of Chicago Press.

Quinney, R. (1970) *The Social Reality of Crime*. Boston, MA: Little, Brown.

Radcliffe-Brown, A. R. (1922) *The Andaman Islanders*. New York, NY: The Free Press, 1964.

Radcliffe-Brown, A. R. (1937) *A Natural Science of Society*. Glencoe: The Free Press, 1957.

Radcliffe-Brown, A. R. (1940) 'On social structure' in A. R. Radcliffe-Brown *Structure and Function in Primitive Society*. London: Cohen and West, 1952.

Radcliffe-Brown, A. R. (1950) 'Introduction' in A. R. Radcliffe-Brown and D. Forde (eds) *African Systems of Kinship and Marriage*. Oxford: Oxford University Press.

Rex, J. A. (1961) *Key Problems of Sociological Theory*. London: Routledge and Kegan Paul.

Rex, J. A. and Moore, R. (1969) *Race, Community and Conflict: A Study of Sparkbrook*, Corrected Edition. London: Oxford University Press.

Richards, A. I. (1957) 'The concept of culture in Malinowski's work' in R. Firth (ed.) *Man and Culture*. London: Routledge and Kegan Paul.

Rivers, W. H. R. (1906) *The Todas of South India*. London: Macmillan.

Rivers, W. H. R. (1924) *Social Organisation*. London: Dawsons of Pall Mall, 1968.

Roberts, M. (1996) *Analytical Marxism: A Critique*. London: Verso.

Robertson, R. (1992) *Globalization: Social Theory and Global Culture*. London: Sage.

Roethlisberger, F. J. and Dickson, W. J. (1939) *Management and the Worker*. Cambridge, MA: Harvard University Press.

Rose, D. and O' Reilly, K. (1998) *The ESRC Review of Government Social Classifications*. London: Office of National Statistics and ESRC.

Rose, N. (1989) *Governing the Soul*. London: Routledge.

Sacks, H. (1965–72) *Lectures on Conversation*. Oxford: Basil Blackwell, 1992.

Said, E. (1978) *Orientalism*. New York, NY: Vintage Books.

Saussure, F. de (1916) *Course in General Linguistics*. New York, NY: McGraw-Hill, 1966.

Sawicki, J. (1991) *Disciplining Foucault: Feminism, Power and the Body*. New York, NY: and London: Routledge.

Schäffle, A. (1875–80) *Bau und Leben des sozialen Körpen*, 4 Volumes. Tübingen: Laupp, 1906.

Schattschneider, E. E. (1960) *The Semi-Sovereign People*. New York, NY: Holt, Rinehart and Winston.

Schutz, A. (1932) *The Phenomenology of the Social World*. London: Heinemann Educational Books, 1972.

Scott, J. (1995) *Sociological Theory: Contemporary Debates*. Cheltenham: Edward Elgar.

Scott, J. (1996) *Stratification and Power: Structures of Class, Status and Command*. Cambridge: Polity Press.

Scott, J. (1997) *Corporate Business and Capitalist Classes*. Oxford: Oxford University Press.

Scott, J. (2000) *Social Network Analysis*, Second Edition. London: Sage.

Scott, W. R. (1995) *Institutions and Organizations*. Beverley Hills, CA: Sage.

Shilling, C. (1993) *The Body and Social Theory*. London: Sage.

Shils, E. A. (1961) 'Centre and periphery' in E. Shils *Centre and Periphery: Essays in Macrosociology*. Chicago, IL: University of Chicago Press, 1975.

Simmel, G. (1890) *Uber sociale Differenzierung*. Leipzig: Duncker und Humblot.

Simmel, G. (1900) *The Philosophy of Money*. London: Routledge and Kegan Paul, 1978.

Simmel, G. (1906) *Religion*. New Haven, CT: Yale University Press, 1997.

Simmel, G. (1908) _Soziologie: Untersuchungen Über die Formen der Vergesselshaftung_. Berlin: Düncker und Humblot, 1968.

Simmel, G. (1909) 'The problem of sociology' in K. Wolff (ed.) (1959) _Essays on Sociology, Philosophy, and Aesthetics by Georg Simmel and Others_. New York, NY: Harper and Row.

Simmel, G. (1917) _Grundlegen der Soziologie_. Berlin: Walter de Gruyter.

So, A. Y. and Chiu, S. W. K. (1995) _East Asia and the World Economy_. Thousand Oaks, CA: Sage Publications.

Somers, M. (1998) ' "We're no angels": realism, rational choice, and relationality in social science', _American Journal of Sociology_, 104: 722–84.

Sorokin, P. (1927) _Social Mobility_. New York, NY: Harper and Brothers.

Spencer, H. (1864) 'The social organism' in H. Spencer _Illustrations of Universal Progress_. New York, NY: D. Appleton and Co., 1873.

Spencer, H. (1873) _The Study of Sociology_. London: Kegan Paul, Trench and Co., 1889.

Spencer, H. (1876) _Principles of Sociology, Volume 1_. London: Williams and Norgate, 1906.

Su, T. (1999) 'Clusters of life spaces and other logics of hegemonic rivalry' in V. Bornschier and C. Chase-Dunn (eds) _The Future of Global Conflict_. Beverley Hills, CA: Sage.

Sydie, R. A. (1987) _Natural Women, Cultured Men_. Milton Keynes: Open University Press.

Taylor, I., Walton, P. and Young, J. (1973) _The New Criminology_. London: Routledge and Kegan Paul.

Tenbruck, F. (1959) 'Formal sociology' in K. H. Wolff (ed.) _Essays on Sociology, Philosophy, and Aesthetics by Georg Simmel and Others_. New York, NY: Harper and Row.

Thompson, D'A. (1917) _On Growth and Form_. Cambridge: Cambridge University Press.

Thrasher, F. (1927) _The Gang_. Chicago, IL: University of Chicago Press.

Tiffin, C. and Lawson, A. (eds) (1994) _De-Scribing Empire_. London: Routledge.

Tönnies, F. (1889) _Community and Association_ (based on the 1912 edition). London: Routledge and Kegan Paul, 1955.

Tönnies, F. (1931) _Einführung in die Soziologie_, extracted in W. J. Cahnman and R. Heberle (eds) (1971) _Ferdinand Toennies, On Sociology: Pure, Applied, and Empirical_. Chicago, IL: University of Chicago Press.

Turner, B. (1996) _The Body and Society_, Second Edition. London: Sage.

Turner, B. S. (1991) 'Recent developments in the theory of the body' in M. Featherstone, M. Hepworth and B. Turner (eds) _The Body: Social Process and Cultural Theory_. London: Sage.

Veblen, T. (1899) _The Theory of the Leisure Class: An Economic Study of Institutions_. New York, NY: Macmillan.

Veblen, T. (1904) *The Theory of Business Enterprise.* New York, NY: Scribner, 1915.

Vergata, A. (1994) 'Herbert Spencer: biology, sociology, and cosmic evolution' in S. Maasan *et al.* (eds) *Biology as Society, Society as Biology: Metaphors.* Dordrecht: Kluwer Academic Press.

Vierkandt, A. (1923) *Gesellshaftslehre: Hauptprobleme der Philosophischen Soziologie.* Stuttgart: F. Enke.

Von Bertalanffy, L. (1973) *General System Theory.* Harmondsworth: Penguin.

Walby, S. (1990) *Theorising Patriarchy.* Oxford: Basil Blackwell.

Wallerstein, I. (1974) *The Modern World System I: Capitalist Agriculture and the Origins of the European World-Economy in the Sixteenth Century.* New York, NY: Academic Press.

Wallerstein, I. (1997) 'Eurocentrism and its avatars: the dilemmas of social science', *New Left Review*, 226: 93–108.

Warner, W. L. (1952) *The Structure of American Life.* Chicago, IL: University of Chicago Press.

Warner, W. L. and Lunt, P. S. (1941) *The Social Life of a Modern Community.* New Haven, CT: Yale University Press.

Wasserman, S. and Faust, K. (1994) *Social Network Analysis: Methods and Applications.* New York, NY: Cambridge University Press.

Weber, M. (1904) ' "Objectivity" in social science and social policy' in M. Weber *The Methodology of the Social Sciences.* New York, NY: The Free Press, 1949.

Weber, M. (1914) 'The economy and the arena of normative and de facto powers' in M. Weber *Economy and Society*, edited by G. Roth and C. Wittich. New York, NY: Bedminster Press, 1968.

Weber, M. (1920) 'Conceptual exposition', in M. Weber *Economy and Society*, edited by G. Roth and C. Wittich. New York, NY: Bedminster Press, 1968.

Wellman, B. (1988) 'Network analysis: from metaphor and method to theory and substance' in B. Wellman and S. D Berkowitz (eds) *Social Structures.* New York, NY: Cambridge University Press.

Wells, A. F. (1970) *Social Institutions.* London: Heinemann.

White, H. C. (1963) *An Anatomy of Kinship.* Englewood Cliffs, NJ: Prentice-Hall.

White, H. C., Boorman, S. A. and Breiger, R. L. (1976) 'Social Structure from Multiple Networks: I', *American Journal of Sociology*, 81: 730–80.

Wiese–Becker (1932) *Systematic Sociology, On the Basis of the Beziehungslehre and Gebildelehre of Leopold von Wiese,* adapted and amplified by Howard P. Becker. New York, NY: Wiley.

Williams, R. (1977) *Marxism and Literature.* Oxford: Oxford University Press.

Williams, R. M. (1960) *American Society: A Sociological Investigation,* Second Edition. New York, NY: Alfred A. Knopf.

Williamson, O. E. (1981) 'The economics of organisation: the transactions costs approach', *American Journal of Sociology*, 87: 548–77.

Williamson, O. E. (1985) *The Economic Institutions of Capitalism*. New York, NY: The Free Press.

Wolff, K. H. (1950) *The Sociology of Georg Simmel*. New York, NY: The Free Press.

Wolff, K. H. and Bendix, R. (1955) *Georg Simmel: Conflict and the Web of Group Affiliations*. New York, NY: The Free Press.

Woodiwiss, A. (1998) *Globalisation, Human Rights and Labour Law in Pacific Asia*. Cambridge: Cambridge University Press.

Wrong, D. (1961) 'The oversocialized concept of man in modern sociology', *American Sociological Review*, 26: 183–93.

Young, J. (1971) *The Drugtakers*. London: McGibbon and Kee.

Zorbaugh, H. (1929) *The Gold Coast and the Slum*. Chicago, IL: University of Chicago Press.

Index

STRUCTURATION

John Parker

- How is structuration central to the social sciences?
- What are the implications of conceptualizing the relation between structure and agency as one of duality or dualism?
- Why was structuration theory invented and what can replace it?

Structuration provides an introduction to this central debate in social theory and helps to explain the historical processes producing structures that shape human social life. Few would dispute that social reality is produced by creative human agents operating in pre-existing structural contexts, but social theorists are divided over how structure and agency are related. John Parker contrasts the views of Bourdieu and Giddens, who uphold duality (identity), with those of the post-structurationists, Archer and Mouzelis, who defend dualism (non-identity). The context and logic of the duality arguments are examined, but it is suggested that Giddens' structuration theory is outdated, and the emphasis is placed on making accessible the positive suggestions of the post-structurationist dualists in relation to actual historical cases. The debate about structuration has important consequences for the way we explain the production and transformation of social structures such as institutions and rules, cultural traditions, patterns of regular behaviour, and distributions of power and inequality. Students and researchers across the social sciences will find this to be a clear and accessible guide to a concept at the heart of social theory.

Contents

c128pp   0 335 20394 9 (Paperback)   0 335 20395 7 (Hardback)

CULTURE
REINVENTING THE SOCIAL SCIENCES

Mark J. Smith

- How has the meaning of culture been reconsidered?
- What impact has this had on approaches to social enquiry?
- Should culture be seen as central to social science?

Over the past three decades there has been a transformation in the ways that social science has been conducted. In order to understand what is happening, we have to explore the implications of a rethinking of the meaning of culture, from a hierarchical system of classification to a contested space. This wide-ranging introduction to the concept of culture examines the ways in which we approach social enquiry, and argues that cultural theory can help to overcome problems in disciplinary and interdisciplinary analysis. Mark J. Smith explores how changes in the meaning of 'culture' have pinpointed key shifts in the way we research society, and draws on contemporary sociology, psychology, politics, geography and the study of crime to consider the ways in which cultural transformation has changed the landscape of social research. He concludes with a persuasive and focused discussion of the centrality of culture in post-disciplinary social science. This landmark text represents essential reading for students and researchers with an interest in the cultural dimension of social science.

Contents
Prologue: Culture and the postdisciplinary imperative – A genealogy of culture: from canonicity to classification – Culture and everyday life: the ordinary is extraordinary – Culture and structure: the logic of mediation – Culture and hegemony: towards the logic of articulation – Contested cultural spaces: identity discourse and the body – Culture and the prospects for a postdisciplinary social science – References – Index.

c144pp   0 335 20318 3 (Paperback)   0 335 20319 1 (Hardback)

DISCOURSE

David Howarth

- What do we mean by discourse?
- What are the different conceptions of discourse and methods of discourse analysis in the contemporary social sciences?
- How can this concept help to clarify key theoretical problems and illuminate empirical cases?

The concept of discourse provokes considerable debate and is understood in a variety of ways in the contemporary social sciences. This text presents a comprehensive overview of the different conceptions and methods of discourse analysis, while setting out the traditions of thinking in which these conceptions have emerged. It surveys structuralist, post-structuralist and post-Marxist theory, and the author sets out a fresh approach to discourse analysis, drawing principally on the writings of Saussure, Lévi-Strauss, Gramsci, Althusser, Foucault, Derrida, Laclau and Mouffe. He evaluates a number of pertinent criticisms of this approach, and explores ways in which discourse analysis can assist our understanding of identity formation, hegemony, and the relationship between structure and agency. This concise and engaging text provides a stimulating introduction to the concept of discourse for students and researchers across the social sciences.

Contents

Introduction:- defining the concept of discourse – Saussure, structuralism and symbolic systems – Post-structuralism, deconstruction and textuality – Foucault's archaeology of discursive practices – Genealogy, power/knowledge and problematization – The limits of ideology in marxist theory – Laclau and Mouffe's theory of discourse – Deploying discourse theory – References – Index.

c128pp   0 335 20070 2 (Paperback)   0 335 20071 0 (Hardback)

SOCIAL DARWINISM

Peter Dickens

- What is the value of evolutionary thought to social theory – and vice versa?
- How has human nature evolved and is it realized or constrained by modern society?
- Are there parallels between social evolution and evolution in the natural world?

Social Darwinism is the extension of Darwin's evolutionary ideas to human society. Over the past two centuries it has been argued that the 'fittest' in terms of physical and mental prowess are the most likely to survive and reproduce. It has also been suggested that the increasingly complex structure of human society mirrors the increasing complexity of nature. This highly original text examines whether these extensions from nature to society are justified, and considers how dangerous they may be in implying the systematic neglect – or even destruction – of the least 'fit'. It asks what, in any case, is 'fitness' as applied to human beings? It also questions whether human nature is constrained by modern society and whether people evolved as essentially competitive or collaborative. Written in a clear and accessible style, with text boxes to explain key ideas and little or no biological knowledge required of the reader, this book suggests a new way in which evolutionary thought and social theory can be combined. Dickens argues that the difficulties and prejudices associated with the field can be avoided by combining historical materialism with aspects of contemporary biology to create a 'Social Darwinism' for the twenty-first century.

Contents
Introduction – Social Darwinism: problems of direction, purpose and progress – Evolutionary thought in contemporary sociology – Nature-Culture dualism and beyond – New forms of social Darwinism: The Bell Curve *and its implications – An evolved human nature? Social Darwinism: Towards a new synthesis – References – Index.*

144pp   0 335 20218 7 (Paperback)   0 335 20219 5 (Hardback)